TAKE YOUR
LOVE
TO YOUR FAMILY AND YOUR
FRUSTRATIONS
TO THE LORD

OTHER COVENANT BOOKS, AUDIO CDs, AND DVDs
BY JOHN LUND:

For All Eternity
The Myth We Call Perfection
Expressions of Love: Intimacy in Marriage
Daughters of Eve
Love One Another
How to Hug a Teenage Porcupine
Bringing Love Home
Without Offense: The Art of Giving and Receiving Criticism
How to Get What You Want from Your Parents
Discovering the Lands of the Book of Mormon
How Do I Love Thee: Understanding Your Spouse's Love Language

OTHER BOOKS
BY JOHN LUND:

How to Hug a Porcupine: Dealing with Toxic and Difficult to Love Personalities
Mesoamerica and the Book of Mormon: Is This the Place?
Joseph Smith and the Geography of the Book of Mormon

TAKE YOUR LOVE
TO YOUR FAMILY AND YOUR
FRUSTRATIONS
TO THE LORD

DR. JOHN L. LUND
& BONNIE LUND

Covenant Communications, Inc.

Cover Image: *Vector Card with a Gold Pattern. Design Elements in a Gothic Style. Perfect for Greetings, Invitations and Announcements* © Lookus, Shutterstock

Published by Covenant Communications, Inc.
American Fork, Utah

Copyright © 2020 by John and Bonnie Lund
All rights reserved. No part of this book may be reproduced in any format or in any medium without the written permission of the publisher, Covenant Communications, Inc., P.O. Box 416, American Fork, UT 84003. This work is not an official publication of The Church of Jesus Christ of Latter-day Saints. The views expressed within this work are the sole responsibility of the author and do not necessarily reflect the position of The Church of Jesus Christ of Latter-day Saints, Covenant Communications, Inc., or any other entity.

Printed in the United States of America
First Printing: February 2020

11 10 9 8 7 6 5 4 3 2

978-1-52440-865-7

*To all those who loved much and did what
they could in loving the difficult to love.*

TABLE OF CONTENTS

Chapter One: When the One You Love Persists in
Making Poor Choices 1

Chapter Two: You Cannot Carry Out the
Lord's Plan in the Devil's Way 5

Chapter Three: God Has a Plan for
You and Your Loved One 31

Chapter Four: Five Principles of
Divine Intervention 67

Chapter Five: Forgiving Increases
Our Ability to Love 105

Chapter Six: How Do I Love Thee? 119

Appendix 137

CHAPTER ONE

WHEN THE ONE YOU LOVE PERSISTS IN MAKING POOR CHOICES

LET'S ASSUME THAT YOUR EXPECTATIONS for your loved one are reasonable and in the personal best interest of your loved one. Let's agree that the loved one knows what you expect but that he or she is unwilling to change. This leaves you frustrated because your loved one's behavior and your expectations don't match. Now the question becomes: how are you going to deal with your frustrations? What does your relationship look like now? If you continue on your current path, what will it look like in the future?

Life gives you two choices. You can act or you can react. You can initiate behaviors toward your loved one, and you can choose how you want to respond to your loved one. If your objective is to change your loved one's behavior, you need to understand your limitations. True change comes from within the person who changes. People will not change their behavior until they come to themselves, as did the prodigal son.

It is easier to understand the parable of the prodigal son if you understand the Jewish culture of Jesus's time. The prodigal son was a wealthy Jewish boy, but he was not the firstborn. According to Jewish law, the firstborn received a double portion for an inheritance so that he could care for his widowed mother and unmarried sisters. In the case of two sons, as was the case in the parable, the older brother would receive two-thirds of the father's inheritance, and the younger brother would receive one-third of the father's inheritance.

A few other cultural insights increase our understanding. First, it's clear that the father was wealthy, because he had many servants, lands, cattle, and goats. Second, Jews were prohibited from eating pork—in fact, by custom, they were prohibited from even being around swine.

After wasting a third of his father's inheritance by "riotous living" in a gentile country with harlots, as his older brother supposed, the younger brother was reduced to feeding pigs and would "have filled his belly with the husks that the swine did eat: and no man gave unto him" (Luke 15:16). After suffering the consequences of his poor choices, he finally "came to himself" (Luke 15:17). The change had to come from inside his own mind and heart.

In many ways, all of us are prodigal children. Some of us learn more quickly than others. We can learn much by observation. Willingly obeying correct principles has its own rewards. However, some of us learn only by enrolling in the school of "hard knocks." We learn by the things we suffer. As the Lord said, "And my people must needs be chastened until they learn obedience, if it must needs be, by the things which they suffer" (D&C 105:6). The prodigal had to learn things by suffering the loss of all his material goods. His change of heart came from within himself.

I have wondered about the conversations the elder brother had with his younger brother before the prodigal son left home. The faithful elder brother had kept all of his father's commandments and was a hard worker. The eldest son surely would have pointed out the foolishness and lack of wisdom displayed by his younger brother. The elder brother obviously would have criticized the character flaws he saw in his younger brother even as he later criticized his father for accepting his brother back home. In defense of the older brother, culturally it was not the practice to take one's inheritance before the death of the father; the prodigal son should not have asked his father for his money while the father was still alive. However, this does not justify the lack of compassion expressed by the elder brother.

The younger brother did not lack knowledge. He was controlled by his pride. His attitude was impaired by selfishness and the kind of short-term thinking that says, *I'm going to do what I want to do when I want to do it, and I don't care what anybody else thinks.* What he lacked that prevented him from making positive choices was real-life experience. It took the loss of everything he possessed, including his pride, before he came to himself.

Once he "came to himself," what was it that drew the prodigal back to his father's side? In addition to the prodigal son's destitute condition, it was his faith in his father's love that drove him home.

Independent of the poor choices a prodigal child or loved one may make, there is something we can do and something the Lord can do. We can take our love to our loved ones and let the Lord be responsible for changing the hearts of those we care about the most. You may ask, "Will the Lord truly intervene? Why hasn't He done so already? What can I do?" It takes faith in Christ along with love and patience, but there is something you can do. Above all, it requires a willingness on your part to "cease to find fault" (D&C 88:124).

There is hope for your loved one to abandon a self-destructive course if you can refrain from inappropriate criticism. Uninspired fault-finding and criticism overwhelm any message of love you may send. Your ability to communicate your love becomes lost when you hinder that message with uninspired criticism. The father of the prodigal son did not harp, control, or nag.

In our opinion, a better title for this parable would be "the parable of a loving father." The real hero in this parable is the father, who demonstrates his love for both of his sons. How many hours did that father spend looking at the distant horizon, hoping that his lost son would return? How many prayers left the heart of that father and found a listening ear and the caring heart of our Heavenly Father? Without question, there were certainly quite a few. When the prodigal son "was yet a great way off, his father saw him, and had compassion, and ran, and fell on his neck, and kissed him" (Luke 15:20). The father's attitude was not one of "I told you so." Rather, the love of the father motivated him to kill the fatted calf, bring forth the best robe, and put a ring on his son's hand and shoes on his feet.

When the elder brother saw his father's affection and generosity, he refused to come to the welcome-home party for his brother. The focus of the older son was the money, the evil choices his brother had made, and the fact that his brother had squandered his inheritance on wicked and riotous living. The scripture records that a loving father reached out to his eldest son as well and confirmed his love for him: "Son, thou art ever with me, and all that I have is thine" (Luke 15:31). The eldest son lost nothing of his own inheritance because of the poor choices of his brother. A robe, a ring, a pair of shoes, and the fatted calf were all the inheritance the youngest son received, and those things were within the purview of a loving father to give.

As correct as they may have been, all the criticisms of the elder brother did not bring about change in the younger brother. The prodigal son was not inspired to come home to a critical brother. The love of his father was what drew the prodigal son home, attracting him like a magnet to his father's heart and home.

The Greatest Motivator

There are three classic motivators: fear, reward, and love. Without question, the greatest motivator of all is love. There is something in each of us that gravitates toward love. It is our firm belief that no one other than the sons of perdition can resist the power of God's infinite love forever. Sooner or later, everyone will be drawn by the pure love of Christ. Every knee will voluntarily bow and every tongue will swear that Jesus is the Christ (see Isaiah 45:23). It would be contrary to the laws of heaven for God to force people to bow the knee. God respects agency. This means that at some point prior to our resurrection, each of us will willingly conform our behaviors to heavenly principles.

As human beings, we have certain fundamental needs that must be met if we are to stay alive. They include, among others, air, food, and water. Next, as children of God, we have a fundamental need for love and belonging. Our Heavenly Father's love is the most important source of love for each of us, something that is true even if we are not consciously aware of it now.

We believe there is a deep, subliminal desire within each of us to return to our heavenly home and to feel our Heavenly Father's love and acceptance. God's love through the Atonement of His Son Jesus Christ already vibrates like a tuning fork within each of our souls, calling us home. Sometimes before we can believe that God can love us we need to be convinced that we are worthy of being loved by someone else. What if you are that someone else?

CHAPTER TWO

YOU CANNOT CARRY OUT THE LORD'S PLAN IN THE DEVIL'S WAY

What Is the Devil's Way?

Satan's ultimate goal is to restrict and take away the agency of the individual and create misery (see Moses 4:3). Lucifer "sought also the misery of all mankind. . . . for he seeketh that all men might be miserable like unto himself" (2 Nephi 2:18, 27). If there is misery in any relationship to which you are a party, that misery can in most cases be traced to trying to do something right in the wrong way.

We are told that the Prophet Enoch saw in vision Satan: "And he beheld Satan; and he had a great chain in his hand, and it veiled the whole face of the earth with darkness; and he looked up and laughed, and his angels rejoiced" (Moses 7:26). Major links in Satan's chain that veils the whole face of the earth are contention, inappropriate and uninspired criticism, and faultfinding. Even inspired criticism given in an inappropriate way creates misery. Satan relies on good intentions carried out in improper ways. The devil is an arch deceiver and a master of justification. It is important to note that "the devil cheateth their souls, and leadeth them away carefully down to hell" (2 Nephi 28:21).

From what we have been able to observe based on five decades of family and marriage counseling, criticism and contention have destroyed more marriages and family relationships than infidelity. The devil will "carefully" try to make you believe that your good intentions justify how you act and what you say. For example, he will convince you that it's okay to be critical because you have good intentions and you love the other person. But unless criticism is given in the Lord's way, misery results. We will describe how to deliver a critical message in the Lord's way a little later.

Critical Dad and His Eighteen-Year-Old Son, Bill

Dad had spent his entire life being critical of his son, Bill. The father believed that his criticisms would help Bill become a better person. They certainly didn't. As a matter of fact, Bill resented his father and labeled him a perfectionist. It wasn't long before Bill avoided his father as much as possible. Bill believed he would never measure up to his father's expectations; in fact, he concluded that even if he did everything his father wanted him to do, it still would not be enough. He wondered why he should do anything his father wanted, because he would still have to deal with being unacceptable to his critical dad.

The father constantly criticized Bill, saying that he needed to be more responsible or he wouldn't amount to anything in this life. Sadly, that was the very narrative that Bill began to believe about himself. *"When the person who professes to love you most finds you unacceptable, then maybe he is right,"* Bill thought. Bill wound up hating his father and all that his father stood for, including the Church. Bill stopped attending church and chose not to serve a mission. Bill will be accountable for his choices, but his father was responsible for giving criticism in the devil's way. Uninspired criticism is one of the devil's most effective tools for creating misery.

Appropriate Criticism

There is such a thing as "appropriate criticism," but it involves specific requirements. The first requirement is that the Holy Ghost inspires the criticism, "Reproving betimes with sharpness, when moved upon by the Holy Ghost" (D&C 121:43). The 1828 Noah Webster's Dictionary, which dates to the time of this revelation, defined *reproof* as "blame expressed to the face; censure for a fault; reprehension." *Betimes* was defined as "seasonably; in good season or time; before it is late." *Sharpness* was defined as "keenness." It meant to be precise, specific, and to the point.

The premise for justifiable criticism is based in the fact that "the powers of heaven cannot be controlled nor handled only upon the principles of righteousness" (D&C 121:36). Inappropriate and uninspired criticism causes "the heavens [to] withdraw themselves; the Spirit of the Lord is grieved" (D&C 121:37). The critical person is left to himself or herself without the help of the Lord. In the example of Bill and his father, the father's criticisms were not inspired by the Holy Ghost. They were inspired by frustration, disappointment, and at times by anger.

The second requirement for giving inspired criticism is the manner in which the criticism is given. How we deliver an inspired critical message is as important as the message itself. Not only does the message have to be appropriate, the delivery system must be equally appropriate. Jesus said, "I am the way, the truth, and the life: no man cometh unto the Father, but by me." (John 14:6). Giving criticism in the Lord's way requires that the critical message be delivered in a way that will not offend the Holy Ghost. Yelling, screaming, and using abusive language will certainly drive the Holy Ghost away. In response, the one being criticized usually cries, pleads, and bemoans, avoiding the supplicant without changing his or her behavior.

Love and convincing the one being criticized that your acceptance is "stronger than the cords of death" (D&C 121:44) will always be accompanied by "showing forth afterwards an increase of love toward him whom thou hast reproved, lest he esteem thee to be his enemy" (D&C 121:43).

Bill was convinced that his father was his enemy. The faultfinding father felt justified in being critical because he loved his son and was frustrated by his son's poor choices and lack of responsibility. The father's evaluation of his son was correct. Bill was irresponsible. The father's intentions were good. How many times have you heard the saying, "The road to hell is paved with good intentions?" The blind spot for the father was his delivery system. The pattern the father had established with his son was criticizing, often in anger, and then apologizing afterward for being angry but justifying the criticism. All Bill heard was the message that he was unacceptable to his father.

Unintentionally, the father had created the perfect scenario for his son to seek acceptance from his dysfunctional friends. Bill's friends offered him unconditional acceptance. The problem was that Bill's friends accepted everything, including drugs, promiscuity, and breaking the laws of the land.

John met with Bill while serving as a Church Educational System instructor at Utah State Prison. Bill was in a twelve-step program to overcome addiction. It wasn't serendipity; it was divine intervention that gave John the opportunity to meet with Bill's parents as a result of speaking at a stake fireside in the Salt Lake area. The parents wanted to know what they could do to help their son in prison. They had been fervently seeking for help. Time had softened the heart of the father, but at that time Bill refused to have his parents visit him. John had the opportunity to visit with Bill's parents on several occasions. He asked, "Are you willing to do what the Lord would have you do to help your son?" They responded with a sincere yes. When the time was right, John was able to share the following advice:

> Don't give one more word of criticism to your son; don't even offer a suggestion as to how he may improve his life. Let go of

trying to change him. Turn him over to the Lord 100 percent. Take your love to Bill, and take your frustrations about Bill to the Lord in mighty prayer. Take to the Lord in prayer every concern, every feeling of disappointment, and every hope you have for Bill. If the Lord opens up the prison doors and you are able to visit with your son, here is what I want you to say to him: "Bill, I have been far too critical of you in my life, and I ask you to forgive me. You will never again hear a critical word from me. In fact, I will not share advice or my opinion unless you ask for it. I love you, son; will you forgive me? You don't have to respond now."

John shared with Bill's parents that when asking for forgiveness it is important not to attempt to explain why you were critical. Explanations come across as justification and cloud the original issue of asking for forgiveness.

Why should Bill's parents have to apologize and ask for forgiveness? Reconciliation requires that each party in a relationship accept responsibility for his or her behaviors. The father's constant uninspired and inappropriate criticism was something the father had to own. Bill was responsible for his poor choices, regardless of having a critical and toxic father.

In the early days of the Church, debt was a major concern. The Prophet Joseph pleaded with the Lord and asked Him what the Church should do about its debts. The Lord's answer was very instructive:

> And again, verily I say unto you, concerning your debts—behold it is my will that you shall pay all your debts.
>
> And it is my will that you shall humble yourselves before me, and obtain this blessing by your diligence and humility and the prayer of faith.
>
> And inasmuch as you are diligent and humble, and exercise the prayer of faith, behold, I will soften the hearts of those to whom you are in debt, until I shall send means unto you for your deliverance. . . .
>
> And inasmuch as ye are humble and faithful and call upon my name, behold, I will give you the victory.
>
> I give unto you a promise, that you shall be delivered this once out of your bondage. (D&C 104:78–80, 82–83)

The Prophet Joseph and others thought that the problem was a lack of money. The Lord informed them that the real problem was the lack of humility, diligence, and the prayer of faith. The Lord promised that according to their humility, diligence, and faith He would divinely intervene and soften the hearts of the creditors. Softening the heart is only one of several options available to the Lord in solving a problem when we invite Him by prayer.

In the Book of Mormon, Amulek underscored the importance of humility, diligence, and the prayer of faith:

> Therefore may God grant unto you, my brethren, that ye may begin to exercise your faith unto repentance, that ye begin to call upon his holy name, that he would have mercy upon you;
>
> Yea, cry unto him for mercy; for he is mighty to save.
>
> Yea, humble yourselves, and continue in prayer unto him.
>
> Cry unto him when ye are in your fields, yea, over all your flocks.
>
> Cry unto him in your houses, yea, over all your household, both morning, mid-day, and evening.
>
> Yea, cry unto him against the power of your enemies.
>
> Yea, cry unto him against the devil, who is an enemy to all righteousness.
>
> Cry unto him over the crops of your fields, that ye may prosper in them.
>
> Cry over the flocks of your fields, that they may increase.
>
> But this is not all; you must pour out your souls in your closets, and your secret places, and in your wilderness.
>
> Yea, and when you do not cry unto the Lord, let your hearts be full, drawn out in prayer unto him continually for your welfare, and also for the welfare of those who are around you. (Alma 34:17–27)

We could add to this scripture, "Cry unto Him over Bill." The parents' humility, prayers, and diligence would then invite the Lord to "divinely intervene" in Bill's life. John asked Bill's parents, "If you knew that Bill would be spiritually well and that Bill's soul would be secure in eternity, would you be willing to cease all criticism and show your acceptance of Bill—not his behavior, but Bill as your son? When appropriate, would you show Bill sincere and heartfelt affection and appreciation? Would you be willing to stop all faultfinding and negative comments to or about Bill?"

As part of John's counseling with them, he told them they were not to make disparaging remarks about Bill to friends or family. They also needed to stop being critical of Bill's friends. If they wanted the Lord's help, they needed to stop being critical. Their job description was simple: Stop all uninspired criticism and love Bill, yet remain persistent in humility, diligence, and the prayer of faith.

Vitally important to this process was their willingness to take their frustrations about Bill to the Lord. They needed to be willing to invite the Lord to divinely intervene in the life of their son. Humility, prayer, and diligence would qualify them before the Lord and bind the Lord with a promise to divinely intervene in Bill's life. If they wanted this whole thing to work, they would need to be cease being critical and exercise patience and trust in the Lord. As Elder Neal A. Maxwell said, "Patient endurance permits us to cling to our faith in the Lord and our faith in His timing."[1]

The Lord will intervene in His own time, and in His own way, and according to His own will (see D&C 88:68). The Lord's plan of redemption extends beyond this mortal life. Paul reminded the Corinthians that "If in this life only we have hope in Christ, we are of all men most miserable" (1 Corinthians 15:19). The Lord's time includes this earth life, the spirit world, and the Millennium.

Joseph Smith passionately taught, "It is not all to be comprehended in this world; it will be a great work to learn our salvation and exaltation even beyond the grave."[2]

This is true for you and for Bill. Be patient and try the Lord's plan. His plan works. Uninspired and improperly given criticism doesn't work. It does not change behavior for the good. Charity involves patience and at some point, long-suffering. You do not have the power to change the heart of your loved one except through prayer and love. God does change His children's minds and hearts consistent with agency, love, and consequences, which are three of the governing principles of this universe.

The hymns of Zion are filled with wisdom and doctrine. Consider the words found in the hymn, "Know This, That Every Soul Is Free." I asked Bill's parents to read it aloud:

> Know this, that ev'ry soul is free
> To choose his life and what he'll be;
> For this eternal truth is giv'n:
> That God will force no man to heav'n.
>
> He'll call, persuade, direct aright,
> And bless with wisdom, love, and light,
> In nameless ways be good and kind,
> But never force the human mind.

---

[1] Neal A. Maxwell, "Endure It Well," *Ensign*, May 1990.
[2] *Teachings of the Prophet Joseph Smith*, sel. Joseph Fielding Smith (Salt Lake City: Deseret Book, 1976), 348.

> Freedom and reason make us men;
> Take these away, what are we then?
> Mere animals, and just as well
> The beasts may think of heav'n or hell.
>
> May we no more our pow'rs abuse,
> But ways of truth and goodness choose;
> Our God is pleased when we improve
> His grace and seek his perfect love. (*Hymns*, no. 240)

I then asked Bill's parents to also ponder the words of the hymn, "Let Us Oft Speak Kind Words":

> Let us oft speak kind words to each other
> At home or where'er we may be;
> Like the warblings of birds on the heather,
> The tones will be welcome and free.
> They'll gladden the heart that's repining,
> Give courage and hope from above,
> And where the dark clouds hide the shining,
> Let in the bright sunlight of love. . . .
>
> Like the sunbeams of morn on the mountains,
> The soul they awake to good cheer;
> Like the murmur of cool, pleasant fountains,
> They fall in sweet cadences near.
> Let's oft, then, in kindly toned voices,
> Our mutual friendship renew,
> Till heart meets with heart and rejoices
> In friendship that ever is true.
>
> Oh, the kind words we give shall in memory live
> And sunshine forever impart.
> Let us oft speak kind words to each other;
> Kind words are sweet tones of the heart. (*Hymns*, no. 232)

Finally, concerning the giving of criticism, faultfinding, and evil speaking, I asked Bill's parents to read the words of the hymn, "Nay, Speak No Ill":

Nay, speak no ill; a kindly word
Can never leave a sting behind;
And, oh, to breathe each tale we've heard
Is far beneath a noble mind.
Full oft a better seed is sown
By choosing thus the kinder plan,
For, if but little good is known,
Still let us speak the best we can.

Give me the heart that fain would hide,
Would fain another's faults efface.
How can it please the human pride
To prove humanity but base?
No, let us reach a higher mood,
A nobler estimate of man;
Be earnest in the search for good,
And speak of all the best we can.

Then speak no ill, but lenient be
To others' failings as your own.
If you're the first a fault to see,
Be not the first to make it known,
For life is but a passing day;
No lip may tell how brief its span.
Then, oh, the little time we stay,
Let's speak of all the best we can. (*Hymns*, no. 233)

Referencing Psalms, the Apostle Peter said, "For he that will love life, and see good days, let him refrain his tongue from evil [speaking], and his lips that they speak no guile" (1 Peter 3:10).

Is There Such a Thing as Inspired Criticism?

There is such a thing as inspired criticism. It is given sparingly and rarely. Two essential characteristics accompany criticism inspired by the Holy Ghost. First, you will be in emotional control; there is no yelling, crying, or cutting words. Second, your tone of voice and even your facial expression will be calm. You will be able to explain your critical concern in sincere words carefully chosen to focus on the inappropriate behavior or choice and not on the worth of the person. You will feel the presence of the Holy Ghost.

There is an axiom that says, "The one who cares the most is held hostage by the one who cares the least." Bill needed to care more about his life than his parents cared. Bill's parents were being held hostage by Bill not caring enough about his own life. In their desire to rescue Bill from his poor choices, they found themselves standing on a mountain top and shouting out warnings about impending disasters, only to be ignored.

It takes practice to escape the natural man and natural woman, both of whom are enemies to God when they speak any of the negative, uninspired thoughts that enter their minds. We become an enemy to God when we destroy the self-worth of another by giving uninspired and uninvited criticism or even valid criticism in an inappropriate way (see Mosiah 3:19). "Remember the worth of souls is great in the sight of God" (D&C 18:10).

Developing a Christlike character will at some point require restraint and self-mastery of the tongue. It is not easy, but it is easier than trying to repair a relationship that has been destroyed by an unbridled tongue. The key for successfully dealing with the frustrations of a loved one who is consistently making poor choices is to take your love to that loved one while taking all of your frustrations about him or her to the Lord in prayer. The exception, of course, is when you are moved upon by the Holy Ghost and your delivery of the criticism does not offend the Holy Ghost.

When communicating acceptance, do not add, "but." The listener will not internalize whatever preceded the "but." When giving praise or asking for forgiveness, any of these "but" statements must remain separate from any other comments. Here is a poor example: "Thank you for cleaning the kitchen, but next time remember to take out the garbage."

Instead, simply say, "Thank you for cleaning the kitchen." Later, at a separate time, ask, "Would you please take out the garbage?"

Mothers frequently tell John, "I don't have time to separate these issues."

His response is to ask them, "How much time do you have to repair a damaged relationship?"

These communication skills are learned behaviors that have to be practiced. And the behaviors have to be consistent with the teachings of Jesus. In the New Testament, the entire third chapter of James is dedicated to controlling the tongue:

> Behold, how great a matter a little fire kindleth!
> And the tongue is a fire . . . and it is set on fire of hell. . . .

Out of the same mouth proceedeth blessing and cursing. My brethren, these things ought not so to be.

. . . but is earthly, sensual, and devilish.

For where envying and strife is, there is confusion and every evil work.

But the wisdom that is from above is first pure, then peaceable, gentle, *and* easy to be entreated, full of mercy and good fruits, without partiality, and without hypocrisy.

And the fruit of righteousness is sown in peace of them that make peace. (James 3:5–18)

A Common Excuse for Giving Criticism

A common excuse for giving criticism is that the criticism is true. However, there is a higher law that states "that which doth not edify is not of God, and is darkness" (D&C 50:23). The natural man lives by the law that says, "I have a mouth and I have a thought and I'm going to say whatever I want to say whenever I want to say it." Critics are certainly free to do so because they have their agency. However, with freedom of speech comes a responsibility to accept the consequences of a glib tongue. King Benjamin warned, "But this much I can tell you, that if ye do not watch yourselves, and your thoughts, and your words . . . ye must perish. And now, O man, remember, and perish not" (Mosiah 4:30).

There is a cautionary saying in the Navy: "Loose lips sink ships." You might also say, "Loose lips sink 'relation–ships.'" Among the consequences of an unbridled tongue are divorce, alienation, rejection, and avoidance of the critic by others.

It is possible to be right about your criticism and wrong in saying it. A wise man once observed that it takes two inspirations to share a criticism. First, one must be inspired that the criticism is true and in the best interest of the one to receive the criticism to hear it at this time. The second inspiration requires that the giver of criticism is calm and able to convey the critical message in a way that focuses on the behavior while reconfirming the worth of the individual who is being criticized.

There is another consideration. All relationships fall into one of three categories. An individual is either in a parent role, such as a parent, boss, or Church leader; a co-equal role, such as a spouse, a sibling, or a neighbor; or in the role of being supervised, such as a child or employee. Language needs to be appropriate to the stewardship. Does the critic have the stewardship and responsibility and therefore the authority to criticize another?

The words that are used should also be appropriate to the stewardship. *Should*, *need*, and *ought* are words that belong to one who has a stewardship over another but are not appropriate for a spouse, because marriage is a relationship of equals. A child should also not tell a parent what the parent *should*, *need*, or *ought* to do. Even when a parent, a boss, or a leader in the Church justifiably uses the words *should*, *need*, or *ought*, the guidelines for giving criticism remain the same. The person must feel inspired by the Holy Ghost and deliver the critical message in a way that does not offend the Holy Ghost.

Permission to Criticize an Equal

It is inappropriate to criticize an equal like a spouse, a co-worker, or a neighbor without their permission. Like it or not, such a person is on an "equal" status with you. Even if you possess superior knowledge, your unbridled tongue announces that you are a law unto yourself, devoid of common courtesy and respect. A mouth and a thought do not give you permission. How would you respond to a co-worker or neighbor who came to you and told you what you should, need, or ought to do? Uninvited criticism is generally responded to with contention or silent rage. Rare is the person who responds to an uninvited criticism with the words, "Thank you for sharing your criticism with me, I'm sure I'll be a better person for it."

Asking for permission to criticize might sound like this: "I have a suggestion that I would like to share. Would this be a good time to do it?"

Uninspired and inappropriately given criticism creates contention, and the devil is the father of contention. Contention is antithetical to the gospel teachings of Jesus and is another tool of the devil to create havoc in a relationship:

> And there shall be no disputations among you, as there have hitherto been; neither shall there be disputations among you concerning the points of my doctrine, as there have hitherto been.
>
> For verily, verily I say unto you, he that hath the spirit of contention is not of me, but is of the devil, who is the father of contention, and he stirreth up the hearts of men to contend with anger, one with another (3 Nephi 11:28–29).

This doesn't mean that people can't disagree or hold opposing opinions. It is how these opinions are expressed that creates contention. When contention is present, the Holy Ghost quietly drifts away, leaving the combatants to revel in their self-imposed misery. The scriptures warn, "beware lest there shall arise contentions among you, and ye list to obey the evil spirit" (Mosiah 2:32). Contention is often the result of poorly given criticism and is a root cause of the destruction of marriages, families, and nations. Regarding the destruction of the Nephites, Mormon noted, "for it has been their quarrelings and their contentions . . . which brought upon them their wars and their destructions" (Alma 50:21).

The early Latter-day Saints were advised to "cease to find fault one with another" (D&C 88:124). The failure of some to follow this counsel resulted in apostasy and contention, and many left the Church. You must handle criticism as you would a deadly herbicide—in your attempt to destroy a weed, you must be careful not to destroy the entire lawn.

After Bill's parents were convinced that criticism poorly given had alienated their son, I shared with them the hope in Christ that their wayward son could, like the prodigal son in the Lord's parable, return home again (see Luke 15:11–32). The Apostle Orson F. Whitney gave a sermon that gives hope to every parent who is willing to follow the Lord's plan of taking your love to your loved one while taking your frustrations to the Lord:

> You parents of the willful and the wayward! Don't give them up. Don't cast them off. They are not utterly lost. The Shepherd will find his sheep. They were his long before they were yours—long before he entrusted them to your care; and you cannot begin to love them as he loves them. They have but strayed in ignorance from the Path of Right, and God is merciful to ignorance. Only the fulness of knowledge brings the fulness of accountability. Our Heavenly Father is far more merciful, infinitely more charitable, than even the best of his servants and the Everlasting Gospel is mightier in power to save than our narrow finite minds can comprehend.
>
> The Prophet Joseph declared—and he never taught more comforting doctrine—that the eternal sealings of faithful parents and the divine promises made to them for valiant service in the cause of truth, would save not only themselves, but likewise their posterity. . . .
>
> Though some of the sheep may wander, the eye of the Shepherd is upon them, and sooner or later they will feel the tentacles of Divine Providence reaching out after them and drawing them back to the fold. Either in this life or the life to come, they will return. They will have to pay their debt to justice; they will suffer for their sins; and may tread a thorny

path; but if it leads them at last, like the penitent Prodigal, to a loving and forgiving father's heart and home, the painful experience will not have been in vain. Pray for your careless and disobedient children; hold on to them with your faith. Hope on; trust on, till you see the salvation of God.

Who are these straying sheep—these wayward sons and daughters? They are the children of the Covenant, heirs to the promises, and have received, if baptized, the gift of the Holy Ghost, which makes manifest the things of God. Could all that go for naught?[3]

The "tentacles of Divine Providence" include the very principles of "divine intervention" we will be discussing. Notice that Apostle Whitney encouraged parents to, in essence, take their frustrations about their wayward children to the Lord in prayer and to hope on and trust in Christ's Atonement. There were promises made by the Lord during our premortal existence, hence the phrase, "heirs to the promises." Parents are equally heirs to a promise conditioned on the parent's willingness to be humble, diligent, and prayerful.

Brigham Young made the following comforting statements to the parents of wayward children:

> Let the father and mother, who are members of this Church and Kingdom, take a righteous course, and strive with all their might never to do a wrong, but to do good all their lives; if they have one child or one hundred children, if they conduct themselves towards them as they should, binding them to the Lord by their faith and prayers, I care not where those children go, they are bound up to their parents by an everlasting tie, and no power of the earth or hell can separate them from their parents in eternity; they will return again to the fountain from whence they sprang.[4]

President Lorenzo Snow challenged parents to consider that their faithfulness would empower them to be saviors on mount Zion for their children:

> If you succeed in passing through these trials and afflictions and receive a resurrection, you will, by the power

---
[3] Conference Report, April 1929, 110.
[4] Brigham Young, *Journal of Discourses*, 11:215.

of the Priesthood, work and labor, as the Son of God has, until you get all your sons and daughters in the path of exaltation and glory. This is just as sure as that the sun rose this morning over yonder mountains. Therefore, mourn not because all your sons and daughters do not follow in the path that you marked out to them, or give heed to your counsels. Inasmuch as we succeed in securing eternal glory, and stand as saviors, and as kings and priests to our God, we will save our posterity.[5]

Elder Boyd K. Packer acknowledged the difficulty of raising children in an immoral society:

> It is a great challenge to raise a family in the darkening mists of our moral environment. . . . It is not uncommon for responsible parents to lose one of their children, for a time, to influences over which they have no control. They agonize over rebellious sons or daughters. They are puzzled over why they are so helpless when they have tried so hard to do what they should. It is my conviction that those wicked influences one day will be overruled. . . .
>
> We cannot overemphasize the value of temple marriage, the binding ties of the sealing ordinance, and the standards of worthiness required of them. When parents keep the covenants they have made at the altar of the temple, their children will be forever bound to them.[6]

There is always accountability before the Lord. Elder David A. Bednar underscored the importance of personal accountability in saying that wayward children will not be automatically saved. They will have to repent and account for their sins at some point in time. Nevertheless, says Elder Bednar, "Faithful parents can invite the power of heaven to influence their children."[7] This means that all of us are responsible for the consequences of our poor choices. No one will escape the need to repent, to appeal to the Lord for forgiveness, and to harmonize their life with the principles of the gospel.

The Prophet Joseph taught:

---

[5] Address delivered October 6, 1893; in *Collected Discourses*, 3:364–365.
[6] "Our Moral Environment," *Ensign*, April 1992.
[7] "Faithful Parents and Wayward Children," *Ensign*, March 2014.

There is never a time when the spirit is too old to approach God. All are within the reach of the pardoning mercy, who have not committed the unpardonable sin. . . . This doctrine appears glorious, inasmuch as it exhibits the greatness of divine compassion and benevolence in the extent of the plan of human salvation.[8]

One by One

It is important to understand that Heavenly Father loves our children more than we do. In general, we refer to a plan of salvation and happiness for all of God's children. In reality, there is an individual plan of salvation and happiness for each one of our Heavenly Father's children.

The doctrine of "one by one" is of paramount importance. Our Heavenly Father has the ability to deal with us as if we were an only child. Jesus is the Only Begotten Son of the Father, but He is not the only "beloved" child of the Father. "All things are present with me, for I know them all" (Moses 1:6). We are often guilty of discounting our Heavenly Father's ability to deal with us as individuals. He knows us all. Jesus also knows us all. When visiting the people on the American continent, Jesus picked up the children and blessed them one by one (see 3 Nephi 17:21).

We partake of the sacrament one by one. We carefully perform each ordinance of the gospel for each and every person in the temples of the Lord. These priesthood ordinances are carried out for one individual at a time. In harmony with the one-by-one principle, the Savior's sacrifice and suffering for us and our sins in the Garden of Gethsemane was done one by one. This doctrine of the Savior atoning for our sins one by one was taught by President Heber J. Grant and other General Authorities. C. S. Lewis is among the most quoted authors in general conference talks. Here is what he said about the Atonement:

> He [Christ] has infinite attention to spare for each one of us. He does not have to deal with us in the mass. You are as much alone with Him as if you were the only being He had ever created. When Christ died, He died for you individually just as much as if you have been the only man in the world.[9]

---

[8] *Teachings of the Prophet Joseph Smith*, 191–192.
[9] Quoted in Tad R. Callister, *The Infinite Atonement* (Salt Lake City: Deseret Book, 2000), 141.

Elder Calister concluded by saying, "The Atonement was ultimately offered for each one of us."[10]

As we pondered on an individual Atonement for each one of our Heavenly Father's children, several scriptures came to our minds. Among them was Alma's declaration, "time only is measured unto men" (Alma 40:8). The Lord in the Garden of Gethsemane was not bound by mortal time when He exercised His divine nature and atoned for all our sins, one child of God at a time. It is something to think about when you partake of the sacrament.

"God works in mysterious ways, his wonders to perform" is not a phrase found in the Bible. It comes from a poem by William Cowper, but it is true.[11] It was the angel Gabriel that informed Mary, "For with God nothing shall be impossible" (Luke 1:37). The words of the prophet Isaiah state, "For my thoughts are not your thoughts, neither are your ways my ways, saith the Lord. For as the heavens are higher than the earth, so are my ways higher than your ways, and my thoughts than your thoughts" (Isaiah 55:8–9).

A Personal Atonement

In trying to explain the Atonement of Jesus Christ or how our Heavenly Father can be omnipresent, the Prophet Joseph taught that the "past, present and future were and are, with Him, one eternal now."[12]

We don't pretend to fully comprehend "how" the Lord atoned for us one by one. We accept it as a matter of faith and by a witness of the Holy Ghost. Imagine for a moment Christ, not bound by time in the Garden of Gethsemane, taking the name of each and every child of God through what might be called the Temple of Gethsemane. What if you were able to see and hear Christ pray to His Heavenly Father and say something like this: "Having authority and acting for and in behalf of Bonnie J. Lund, I take upon myself all her sins and pray, Father, that thou wilt forgive her as I willingly suffer the consequences of her sins. Amen."

How great that suffering must have been if it caused Christ to bleed at every pore of His body (see D&C 19:18, Mosiah 3:7, and Luke 22:44). By the operation of an eternal law, our Savior had the ability to atone for each one of us, one by one, as if we were an only child. We believe that Christ was motivated by love to suffer and sacrifice His life for us individually, even though we do not fully comprehend the eternal laws that govern the atoning sacrifice of Christ.

---

[10] Callister, 142.
[11] "God Moves in a Mysterious Way," 1774.
[12] *Teachings of the Prophet Joseph Smith*, 220.

We know that Christ had a power over death that was given Him by virtue of His unique birth as the Son of God.

> Therefore doth my Father love me, because I lay down my life, that I might take it again.
>
> No man taketh it from me, but I lay it down of myself. I have power to lay it down, and I have power to take it again. This commandment have I received of my Father. (John 10:17–18)

> . . . there can be nothing which is short of an infinite atonement which will suffice for the sins of the world. (Alma 34:12)

So it is that our loving and merciful Heavenly Father has prepared a way through the Atonement of His Son, Jesus Christ, for each of His children to return to Him (see Moses 1:39). Sons of perdition are the exception.

> For all the rest shall be brought forth by the resurrection of the dead, through the triumph and the glory of the Lamb, who was slain, who was in the bosom of the Father before the worlds were made.
>
> And this is the gospel, the glad tidings, which the voice out of the heavens bore record unto us—
>
> That he came into the world, even Jesus, to be crucified for the world, and to bear the sins of the world, and to sanctify the world, and to cleanse it from all unrighteousness;
>
> That through him all might be saved whom the Father had put into his power and made by him;
>
> Who glorifies the Father, and saves all the works of his hands, except those sons of perdition who deny the Son after the Father has revealed him.
>
> Wherefore, he saves all except them. . . . (D&C 76:39–44)

A Latter-day Saint's Understanding of Hell

Our mortal minds have not yet probed the depths of the love and mercy granted to mankind through the Atonement of Jesus Christ. Even those who are guilty of first degree murder may find forgiveness. The Prophet Joseph declared that even King David—who was guilty of the first-degree, cold-blooded murder of Uriah—will ultimately be forgiven, but not on earth. David will be allowed to enter the kingdom of heaven, albeit a lesser degree of glory then what he might have otherwise obtained. David's pathway to the kingdom of heaven goes directly through hell. This means that he could not simply receive forgiveness by asking for it on earth, but he had to go to hell in the spirit world and suffer for his sins. Joseph said that "David sought repentance at the hand of God carefully with tears for the murder of Uriah; but he could only get it through hell: he got a promise that his soul should not be left in hell."[13] Psalm 16, written by David, states, "Therefore my heart is glad, and my glory rejoiceth: my flesh also shall rest in hope. For thou wilt not leave my soul in hell . . ." (Psalm 16:9–10).

Our hope is that our wayward children will come to their senses in this life. However, for the rebellious child who dies in his or her sins, the Lord has prepared a place such a person can seriously consider the consequences of his or her poor choices. That place is called "hell." If one dies unrepentant of sins, the wayward soul will be exposed to Lucifer and others existing in a state of misery. The "preparator of hell" is the Lord, not the devil. "And a hell I have prepared for them, if they repent not," the Lord told Enoch (Moses 6:29).

For a member of The Church of Jesus Christ of Latter-day Saints, "hell" can be a state of mind on earth as well as an actual place in the spirit world. Hell in the spirit world will eventually be empty because Christ conquers death, hell, and the grave (see Revelation 20:13). Those who go to hell as stubborn and unrepentant sinners will eventually come to themselves, as did the prodigal son, after suffering the consequences of their sins and poor choices in mortality. Except for the sons of perdition, the repentant in the spirit-world hell will come forth clean and spotless and be resurrected to a degree of glory in the kingdom of God, after they have suffered for their sins and have learned what they needed to learn in hell. No one will come forth from hell until he or she has paid the utmost farthing (see Matthew 5:26). There are at least eight scriptures that declare that no unclean thing can enter the kingdom of heaven. The heavenly kingdom of God is comprised of degrees of glory referred to as the telestial, terrestrial, and celestial kingdoms (see D&C 76:50–119).

The spirit-world hell will eventually be empty because the sons of perdition will be cast out of hell to outer darkness, where they can exercise their agency without bothering the rest of Heavenly Father's children. They will remain in a hell of their own creation in outer darkness, because they want wickedness to be

---

[13] *Teachings of the Prophet Joseph Smith*, 339.

happiness and it never can be (see Alma 41:10). The Prophet Joseph taught, "A man is his own tormenter and his own condemner. Hence the saying, they shall go into the lake that burns with fire and brimstone."[14]

Because of the Atonement of Jesus Christ, "death and hell" will deliver up the dead that are in them (see Revelation 20:13–14). Even those in hell can be candidates for the heavenly kingdom of God. Elder James E. Talmage taught the Latter-day Saint understanding of hell:

> Many other great truths not known before, have been declared to the people, and one of the greatest is that to hell there is an exit as well as an entrance. Hell is no place to which a vindictive judge sends prisoners to suffer and to be punished principally for his glory; but it is a place prepared for the teaching, the disciplining of those who failed to learn here upon the earth what they should have learned. True, we read of everlasting punishment, unending suffering, eternal damnation. That is a direful expression; but in his mercy the Lord has made plain what those words mean. "Eternal punishment," he says, is God's punishment, for he is eternal; and that condition or state or possibility will ever exist for the sinner who deserves and really needs such condemnation [sons of perdition]; but this does not mean that the individual sufferer or sinner is to be eternally and everlastingly made to endure and suffer. No man will be kept in hell longer than is necessary to bring him to a fitness for something better. When he reaches that stage the prison doors will open and there will be rejoicing among the hosts who welcome him into a better state. The Lord has not abated in the least what he has said in earlier dispensations concerning the operation of his law and his gospel, but he has made it clear unto us his goodness and mercy is through it all, for it is his glory and his work to bring about the immortality and eternal life of man.[15]

Not all go to the spirit-world hell when they die. Those who repent on earth as mortals go to that part of the spirit world known as paradise:

> Now, concerning the state of the soul between death and the resurrection—Behold, it has been made known unto me

---

[14] *Teachings of the Prophet Joseph Smith*, 357.

[15] James E. Talmage, Conference Report, April 1930, 97.

> by an angel, that the spirits of all men, as soon as they are departed from this mortal body, yea, the spirits of all men, whether they be good or evil, are taken home to that God who gave them life.
>
> And then shall it come to pass, that the spirits of those who are righteous are received into a state of happiness, which is called paradise, a state of rest, a state of peace, where they shall rest from all their troubles and from all care, and sorrow. (Alma 40:11–12)

Some lessons can be learned by observation. There are some lessons in life and in the spirit world that we learn only by the things that we suffer (see D&C 105:6). The prodigal son had to come "to himself" (Luke 15:17). He had to learn the hard way, by suffering the natural consequences of his own poor choices (see Luke 15:11–32). Notice that the father's role was to love his son, to bring forth the best robe, to put a ring on his hand, to put shoes on his feet, to kill the fatted calf, and to make a great supper. The prodigal son had lost his inheritance but not his father's love. While the son was yet a great way off, the father saw his son and had compassion and ran and fell on his neck and kissed him.

Love versus Trust

We can take our love to our loved ones without trusting them. There is a distinction between love and trust. It is possible to love someone and not trust them. It is also true that one can forgive another's trespasses and still not trust them. Love is a gift, but trust must be earned by responsible behavior.

As parents, we had a thirteen-year-old we trusted and an eighteen-year-old we didn't trust at that time. We made it clear to our children that our love was infinite and eternal. At the same time, we told them that our trust depended on them being where they said they were going to be and doing what they said they would be doing.

Bill's parents understood that loving their son meant they would help him become his highest and best self, but they would not enable him in a self-destructive course. Putting it another way, "I will support all of your good choices to the best of my ability, but I will not help you one inch to hell."

The Lord's time is not always as soon as we would like it to be. Elder Neal A. Maxwell advised members of the Church to say not only "Thy will be done," but also "Thy timing be done."[16]

---

[16] Neal A. Maxwell, "Glorify Christ," Address to CES Educators, February 2, 2001.

But in this case, the Lord softened Bill's heart so that he allowed for a visit from his parents in just two weeks. Those two weeks involved Bill's parents praying for the Lord to soften Bill's heart and to bless them as parents to be able to communicate their love for their son. I rehearsed with Bill's parents the importance of the father in particular asking for forgiveness from his son.

Bill was upset with his mother because he felt that she didn't protect him from the constant criticism of his father, and therefore she was implicit in the criticism. The mother was able to say, "Bill, I too am asking you to forgive me."

It is difficult to describe the emotional flood of tears that resulted from that meeting with the estranged parents and their jailed son. There were no recriminations, no "I told you so," no blame, and no accusations. There was a great outpouring of love. Hearts were softened on both sides. Bill has a hard road ahead of him. Now, however, he has the love and the emotional support as well as the prayers of his parents.

This very important outcome was the result of the parent's willingness to be humble, diligent, and exercise the prayer of faith whereby they invited God to solve what appeared to be an impossible situation. Our Heavenly Father is very good at divinely intervening and solving impossible problems when He is invited.

Why Do We Have to Pray?

The importance of prayer cannot be overstated. Prayer is an eternal form of communication between us and our Heavenly Father when we are out of His immediate presence. President John Taylor said that we prayed as pre-mortal spirits. It continues on earth and into the spirit world; even resurrected beings pray.

As mortals, we are commanded to pray. On being driven from the Garden of Eden, Adam was commanded to "call upon God in the name of the Son forevermore" (Moses 5:8). The brother of Jared was chastened for more than three hours by the Lord "because he remembered not to call upon the name of the Lord" (Ether 2:14). The same brother of Jared said, "O Lord, thou hast given us a commandment that we must call upon thee, that from thee we may receive according to our desires" (Ether 3:2). The Lord's Prayer came when of one of the Lord's disciples pleaded with Him, "Lord, teach us to pray" (Luke 11:1).

Prayer also exists in the spirit world. The Lord told Cain, "The voice of thy brother's blood cries unto me from the ground" (Moses 5:35). In the Book of Mormon, we find the resurrected Christ praying (see 3 Nephi 19:19–23). Prayer is an eternal principle.

Prayer and agency are intimately intertwined. There is an eternal law regarding God's respect for agency (see Moses 4:3). God can divinely intervene when invited by prayer to do so as long as it is righteous. We are commanded to pray and invite the Lord to help us and our loved ones. As parents, we have the stewardship to teach and instruct our children (see D&C 68:25). We also have the authority to invite our Heavenly Father to divinely intervene in the lives of our children, regardless of their ages. Heavenly Father respects laws, boundaries, and agency. Our prayers authorize Him to divinely intervene in our stewardship in ways that we may not have thought about before.

We know that the powers of heaven are inseparably connected to the principles of righteousness (see D&C 121:36). Prayer is a righteous principle and it gives us access to the powers of heaven. God has given us agency, and He has given us commandments to pray, but we have the option to keep or reject that commandment. There are consequences for obedience and for disobedience (see Deuteronomy 28:1–68). Would it not be a tragedy for you to discover that your prayers could have helped a loved one but you chose not to pray? The scriptures proclaim that an "evil spirit teacheth not a man to pray, but teacheth him that he must not pray" (2 Nephi 32:8). Worthiness is not required by the Lord in order to pray. Just as repentance is a continuous process, we are all unworthy in one way or another at any given time. The issue of worthiness will be dealt with later in this chapter.

Think of the Power in Prayer

The people of Ammonihah were told,

> Yea, and I say unto you that if it were not for the prayers of the righteous, who are now in the land, that ye would even now be visited with utter destruction; yet it would not be by flood, as were the people in the days of Noah, but it would be by famine, and by pestilence, and the sword.
>
> But it is by the prayers of the righteous that ye are spared. (Alma 10:22–23)

Captain Moroni said,

> And there had been murders, and contentions, and dissensions, and all manner of iniquity among the people of

Nephi; nevertheless for the righteous' sake, yea, because of the prayers of the righteous, they were spared. (Alma 62:40)

The Prophet Enos is a great study in prayer. First his soul hungered, and he cried mightily to the Lord for his own soul. Receiving an assurance that his sins had been forgiven, his guilt was swept away. The focus of his prayers changed to the Nephites, his brethren, and he prayed mightily for them. Next the Lord assured him that the Nephites would be blessed as they kept the commandments of the Lord. Feeling confident, Enos prayed many long hours for the Lamanites. The Lord told Enos that He would grant unto him according to his desires because of his faith. Finally, Enos prayed that the record we know as the Book of Mormon might be preserved by the Lord's holy arm (see Enos 1:3–16).

The Lord told the Prophet Joseph Smith after the Book of Mormon came forth,

> And, behold, all the remainder of this work does contain all those parts of my gospel which my holy prophets, yea, and also my disciples, desired in their prayers should come forth unto this people.
>
> And I said unto them, that it should be granted unto them according to their faith in their prayers. (D&C 10:46–47)

"The effectual fervent prayer of a righteous man [and woman] availeth much," said the Apostle James (James 5:16). He also counseled any who were sick to call for the elders of the Church to anoint him with oil and "pray over him. . . . And the prayer of faith shall save the sick, and the Lord shall raise him up; and if he have committed sins, they shall be forgiven him. . . . pray one for another, that ye may be healed" (James 5:14–16).

God Will Not Cease to Be God

We remember being shocked to even think that "God would cease to be God" (Alma 42:22), which Alma explained to his wayward son Corianton regarding mercy robbing justice. Our Heavenly Father abides by eternal laws. He respects those laws, and therein lies His power. It was God Himself who said, "I, the Lord, am bound when ye do what I say; but when ye do not what I say, ye have no promise" (D&C 82:10).

How is the Lord bound? He is bound by eternal law. In *Lectures on Faith* (p. 41), there are certain characteristics assigned to God. Among those characteristics is that God is the same yesterday, today, and forever. He is no respecter of persons, but in every nation he that fears God and works righteousness is accepted. Lastly, He is a God of love.

One of the summation points in Lecture Three is that we have current access to God as much as any former child of God from the time of Adam. We can rely on the consistency of God. He is available to hear our prayers as much as the prayers of any prophets or Apostles. God will not cease to be God. Your prayers count.

God respects agency. Heavenly Father's respect for agency extends even to the sons of perdition. As mentioned, even they will ultimately be allowed their agency in outer darkness. However, when we invite our Heavenly Father by prayer, He does a lot to influence His children so that they can return to Him. But God will not take away their agency.

It is obvious that the Lord allows man's inhumanity to man. He will tolerate for a time the suffering of His children that they may learn to experience the consequences of breaking the law. However, there comes a point beyond which the Lord cannot tolerate wickedness. Without violating the agency of man, God can create an environment for change.

> O, ye nations of the earth, how often would I have gathered you together as a hen gathereth her chickens under her wings, but ye would not!
>
> How oft have I called upon you by the mouth of my servants, and by the ministering of angels, and by mine own voice, and by the voice of thunderings, and by the voice of lightnings, and by the voice of tempests, and by the voice of earthquakes, and great hailstorms, and by the voice of famines and pestilences of every kind, and by the great sound of a trump, and by the voice of judgment, and by the voice of mercy all the day long, and by the voice of glory and honor and the riches of eternal life, and would have saved you with an everlasting salvation, but ye would not! (D&C 43:24–25)

When God takes people to the spirit world, they take their agency with them. God does not take away their agency, but He can certainly change their environment.

What is true for a nation is also true for the individual child of God. Our Heavenly Father will extend every effort to encourage, entice, invite, and when necessary allow the consequences of poor choices to wreak self-inflicted havoc and misery in our lives.

It is important to remember that we are on this earth for a purpose. After obtaining a mortal body, we are here to learn to choose good over evil. If an individual child of God or nation becomes so corrupt that the children have no chance to escape from the incessant and relentless onslaught of evil, God will remove the wicked to the spirit world. The scriptures refer to this as being "ripe in iniquity" or "past feeling" on earth. When an individual is "past feeling" their conscience or a witness from the Holy Ghost or the words of the scriptures or the words of the living prophets and that person then pursues his or her own carnal nature, he or she is "ripe in iniquity." When such a person is removed to the spirit world, it will not be out of hate, but out of love. The flood at the time of Noah was an act of love:

> Behold, the Lord esteemeth all flesh in one; he that is righteous is favored of God. But behold, this people had rejected every word of God, and they were ripe in iniquity; and the fulness of the wrath of God was upon them. (1 Nephi 17:35)

> [To Laman and Lemuel:] Ye are swift to do iniquity but slow to remember the Lord your God. Ye have seen an angel, and he spake unto you; yea, ye have heard his voice from time to time; and he hath spoken unto you in a still small voice, but ye were past feeling, that ye could not feel his words; . . . why is it, that ye can be so hard in your hearts? (1 Nephi 17:45–46)

The people who drowned during the flood at the time of Noah were described in Genesis: "And God saw that the wickedness of man was great in the earth, and that every imagination of the thoughts of his heart was only evil continually" (Genesis 6:5).

How was the flood an act of love? The wicked were removed to the spirit world so that they could learn what they failed to learn on earth. Remaining in their wicked state, they could not spiritually progress. It was a blessing to remove them to the spirit world where they could rethink the consequences of sin.

The righteous at the time of Noah were taken up to the heavenly Zion and avoided the flood: "And Enoch beheld angels descending out of heaven, bearing testimony of the Father and Son; and the Holy Ghost fell on many, and they were caught up by the powers of heaven into Zion" (Moses 7:27).

It is also true that the Lord will at times remove a righteous person by death or translation because that person is needed in the spirit world or in the heavenly Zion. Sometimes a righteous person is removed from the earth to spare him or her from the evil to come. So spoke the Prophet Isaiah: "The righteous perisheth, and no man layeth it to heart: and merciful men are taken away, none considering that the righteous is taken away from the evil to come" (Isaiah 57:1).

Most of us as mortals consider death to be a tragedy. In truth, death is a rite of passage and an essential part of God's plan. After patience and long-suffering followed by the warning voices of prophets, conscience, and witnesses of the Holy Ghost, a people ripe in iniquity will be swept from off the surface of the earth by flood, war, pestilence, or famine. They will be surprised to find themselves in the spirit world, where they can reevaluate their choices between good and evil.

It is worthy of note that during the three days that Jesus was in the spirit world, following His Crucifixion and prior to His Resurrection, He organized the missionary effort to teach those who were rebellious during the days of Noah (see D&C 138:30; 1 Peter 3:18–20). That doesn't sound like an angry God. It does sound like a loving Lord who is looking for the opportunity to help each child of God to grow and progress while respecting the agency of each one.

Now is the opportunity in mortality for us to invite the Lord to divinely intervene through our humility, diligence, and the prayer of faith into the lives of our loved ones.

CHAPTER THREE

GOD HAS A PLAN FOR YOU AND YOUR LOVED ONE

THE PRINCIPLES OF DIVINE INTERVENTION, as they relate to us here on earth, are designed to guide and direct God's children back to Him. God is not some far-removed ideal sitting on a throne with an occasional curiosity about this earth. Our Heavenly Father has a full and comprehensive knowledge of each of His children and has designed a plan of happiness for each and every child.

Because of the Restoration of the gospel, members of The Church of Jesus Christ of Latter-day Saints have been given access to ancient scriptures like the Book of Mormon and the Pearl of Great Price. In conjunction with the Bible, these scriptures shed a great deal of light on God's plan.

The Prophet Joseph Smith shared how intimately our God is involved in each of our lives:

> The great Jehovah contemplated the whole of the events connected with the earth, pertaining to the plan of salvation, before it rolled into existence, or ever "the morning stars sang together" for joy; the past, the present, and the future were and are, with Him, one eternal now. He knew of the fall of Adam, the iniquities of the antediluvians, of the depth of iniquity that would be connected with the human family, their weakness and strength, their power and glory, apostasies, their crimes, their righteousness and iniquity; He comprehended the fall of man, and his redemption; He knew the plan of salvation and pointed it out; He was acquainted with the situation of all nations and with their destiny; He ordered all things according to the council of His own will; He knows the situation of both the living and the dead, and has made ample provision for their redemption, according

to their several circumstances, and the laws of the kingdom of God, whether in this world, or in the world to come.[17]

There is something intuitive in each of our hearts that testifies of a Divine Being who is in control of this universe. The prophet Alma said it best: "all things denote there is a God; yea, even the earth, and all things that are upon the face of it, yea, and its motion, yea, and also all the planets which move in their regular form do witness that there is a Supreme Creator" (Alma 30:44).

In teaching us how to pray, Jesus identified our relationship with God as familial and one of kinship, calling God "Our Father."

> Our Father which art in heaven, Hallowed be thy name.
> Thy kingdom come. Thy will be done in earth, as it is in heaven.
> Give us this day our daily bread.
> And forgive us our debts, as we forgive our debtors.
> And lead us not into temptation, but deliver us from evil: For thine is the kingdom, and the power, and the glory, for ever. Amen. (Matthew 6:9–13). (Matthew 6:14, JST, amends this to read, "And suffer us not to be led into temptation.")[18]

The Apostle Paul observed,

> Furthermore we have had fathers of our flesh which corrected us, and we gave them reverence: shall we not much rather be in subjection unto the Father of spirits, and live? (Hebrews 12:9)

Our relationship with God is intimate. He is literally the Father of our spirit bodies. We celebrate this reality in our hymn, "I Am a Child of God." We understand that we have Heavenly Parents.

We also learn that God has a plan and a purpose for us as His children, a plan that included a premortal existence.

We lived with our Heavenly Parents for eons of time before we were born on this earth. The period prior to our birth in mortality is referred to as our "first estate" (Abraham 3:26). This earth life and subsequent experience after death in the

---

[17] *Teachings of the Prophet Joseph Smith*, 220.
[18] Joseph Smith Translation, Matthew 6:13 (in Matthew 6:13, footnote *a*).

spirit world and to the end of the Millennium is identified as our "second estate." Elder Boyd K. Packer agreed with Alma in referring to Heavenly Father's plan of salvation as a great plan of happiness. Elder Packer compared God's plan to a three-act play.

> There are three parts to the plan. You are in the second or the middle part, the one in which you will be tested by temptation, by trials, perhaps by tragedy . . . The plan of redemption, with its three divisions, might be likened to a grand three-act play. Act 1 is entitled "Premortal Life." The scriptures describe it as our first estate (see Jude 1:6; Abraham 3:26, 28). Act 2, from birth to the time of resurrection, is the "Second Estate." And act 3 is called "Life After Death" or "Eternal Life."
>
> In mortality, we are like actors who enter a theater just as the curtain goes up on the second act. We have missed act 1. The production has many plots and subplots that interweave, making it difficult to figure out who relates to whom and what relates to what, who are the heroes and who are the villains. It is further complicated because we are not just spectators; we are members of the cast, on stage, in the middle of it all![19]

What Do We Know about the Premortal Existence, or Act One?

Frankly, we know a great deal. The poet William Wordsworth captured thoughts about our premortal heavenly home in his poem, "Ode: Intimations of Immortality from Recollections of Early Childhood":

> Our birth is but a sleep and a forgetting:
> The Soul that rises with us, our life's Star, Hath had elsewhere its setting, And cometh from afar: Not in entire forgetfulness, And not in utter nakedness, But trailing clouds of glory do we come from God, who is our home.

The motivation of our Heavenly Father was not much different than that of mortal parents who want to help each of their children reach their highest and best potential. The plan was consistent with the individual premortal

---

[19] "The Plan and the Play," CES Fireside for Young Adults, May 7, 1995.

adult spirit agreeing to accept the opportunities and responsibilities of coming to this earth to obtain a mortal body and experience an eventual resurrection. In addition to obtaining a mortal body, our earth life experience would include a test of our agency. We were to be as God in knowing good and evil (see Moses 4:28). More precisely, we were to learn to discern the difference between good and evil. How would we treat one another once we were out of the immediate presence of God?

During our premortal existence, the time arrived for assignments to be made regarding when and where we were going to come to this earth. God's work is to bring to pass the immortality and eternal life of His children (see Moses 1:39). Consistent with God's plan to assist each soul in becoming his or her highest and best self, various callings were extended to each of us to assist our Heavenly Father in bringing about His work and His glory.

What Does Calling and Election Mean?

Extending an invitation to come to the earth and accept an earthly mission is referred to as the doctrine of "calling." Asking those of us present in the premortal existence during the Grand Council to support each individual "called" is known as the doctrine of "election" or the "sustaining vote." Together they are referred to as the doctrine of "calling and election." These are mentioned by Peter in the New Testament: "brethren, give diligence to make your calling and election sure: for if ye do these things, ye shall never fall" (2 Peter 1:10).

Calling and election is a premortal doctrine and involves the Grand Council in Heaven, in which assignments were made to come to this earth. In a poem published in the *Times and Seasons* in February 1843, the Prophet Joseph Smith indicated that the Grand Council in Heaven was held on the planet Kolob: "From the Council in Kolob, to time on the earth."

> The doctrine of a premortal "calling" is best understood as a divine invitation to serve. These were calls of a voluntary nature that respected the agency of the one being invited. The Apostle Paul reminded Timothy that God "who hath saved us, and called us with a holy calling, not according to our works, but according to his own purpose and grace, which was given us in Christ Jesus before the world began (see 2 Timothy 1:9).
>
> The premortal callings were extended as a part of a great plan of salvation and happiness that had as its stated purpose

"to bring to pass the immortality and eternal life of man" (Moses 1:39).

The prophet Isaiah saw in heavenly vision his own premortal calling, which he reported as follows: "Also I heard the voice of the Lord, saying, Whom shall I send, and who will go for us? Then said I, Here am I; send me" (Isaiah 6:8).

In that Grand Council, our Heavenly Father extended a call for the most important and sacred assignment of them all. The call was to be the Redeemer of the world, the Savior of all mankind, and the "Anointed One." It would be the responsibility of the Anointed One to fulfill the requirements of a priesthood assignment referred to as the Atonement. *Messiah* in Hebrew and *Christos* or *Christ* in Greek means the "Anointed One." The magnitude and eternal significance of this greatest and supernal assignment involved the overcoming of physical and spiritual death. It was by any measure the most important call.

As with all premortal callings, it was not enough to volunteer for the extended call. Each calling had to be supported by those in attendance and by those affected by the various callings. This is the doctrine of "election" or the "sustaining vote." To be called was one issue; to be elected and sustained was quite another matter. The scriptures indicate that more than one person might volunteer to fulfill a calling:

> And the Lord said: Whom shall I send? And one [Christ] answered like unto the Son of Man: Here am I, send me. And another [Lucifer] answered and said: Here am I, send me. And the Lord said: I will send the first.
> And the second was angry, and . . . at that day, many followed after him. (Abraham 3:27–28)

Lucifer became known as the devil. On the Isle of Patmos, John saw this event in vision and recorded the following:

> And there was war in heaven: Michael and his angels fought against the dragon; and the dragon fought and his angels,
> And prevailed not; neither was their place found any more in heaven.
> And the great dragon was cast out, that old serpent, called the Devil, and Satan, which deceiveth the whole

world: he was cast out into the earth, and his angels were cast out with him. (Revelation 12:7–9)

The decision as to who would become the Messiah was put to a sustaining vote. Joseph Smith observed:

> The contention in heaven was—Jesus said there would be certain souls that would not be saved; and the devil said he could save them all, and laid his plans before the Grand Council, who gave their vote in favor of Jesus Christ. So the devil rose up in rebellion against God, and was cast down, with all who had put up their heads for him.[20]

Again it was Peter who reminded the early members of the Church that they were "Elect according to the foreknowledge of God the Father" (1 Peter 1:2). Being called and elected was a wonderful thing and demonstrated the confidence that God and our kindred spirits had in us. It should be humbling to each of us to think that we were selected and sustained by a multitude of the heavenly host.

Consistent with the principles of calling and election is the doctrine of "foreordination." Peter pointed out that Christ "was foreordained before the foundation of the world, but was manifest in these last times for you" (1 Peter 1:20).

After a person had been "called and elected" by the Father and sustained by the General Council in Heaven to serve here on the earth in various offices and callings, that person was preauthorized or foreordained for an earthly mission. Just as members of the Church are ordained to different callings in the Church or are given a patriarchal blessing, so also we were foreordained in our premortal life. At the April 1844 general conference of the Church, Joseph Smith spoke to the Saints and informed them that:

> Every man who has a calling to minister to the inhabitants of the world was ordained to that very purpose in the Grand Council of heaven before this world was. I suppose that I was ordained to this very office in that Grand Council.[21]

Abraham was told by the Lord, "thou wast chosen before thou wast born" (Abraham 3:23). The Prophet Jeremiah was given a similar message:

---

[20] *Teachings of the Prophet Joseph Smith*, 357.
[21] *Teachings of the Prophet Joseph Smith*, 365.

> Then the word of the Lord came unto me, saying,
> Before I formed thee in the belly I knew thee; and before thou camest forth out of the womb I sanctified thee, and I ordained thee a prophet unto the nations. (Jeremiah 1:4–5)

President Joseph F. Smith saw in vision the premortal callings that were extended in the Grand Council in Heaven. Among them were regular members of the Church in this dispensation (see D&C 138:57). It was given to President Smith to understand that many of the callings that were extended and to which people were foreordained included a mission to the spirit world after we departed this mortal life, a mission where we would continue to proclaim the gospel of Jesus Christ. By this we understand that callings and elections to which we were foreordained included not only those during this mortal life but also during our experience in the spirit world and undoubtedly during the Millennium.

> I observed that they were also among the noble and great ones who were chosen in the beginning to be rulers in the Church of God.
> Even before they were born, they, with many others [you and I], received their first lessons in the world of spirits [premortal existence] and were prepared to come forth in the due time of the Lord to labor in his vineyard for the salvation of the souls of men.
> I beheld that the faithful elders of this dispensation, when they depart from mortal life, continue their labors in the preaching of the gospel of repentance and redemption. (D&C 138:55–57)

There are many biblical references to the doctrine of "foreordination," which is a part of the greater doctrine of "calling and election." Consistent with our agency and our willingness, we were assigned by our Heavenly Father to come to this earth at a specific time, that we might fulfill the assignments we were given in the premortal world. Paul alluded to this when he taught:

> God that made the world and all things therein, seeing that he is Lord of heaven and earth . . . hath made of one blood all nations of men for to dwell on all the face of the earth, and hath determined the times before appointed, and the bounds of their habitation. (Acts 17:24, 26)

Job proclaimed, "Man that is born of a woman is of few days, and full of trouble. . . . Seeing his days are determined, the number of his months are with thee, thou [God] hast appointed his bounds that he cannot pass" (Job 14:1, 5).

Moses declared, "When the most High divided to the nations their inheritance, when he separated the sons of Adam, he set the bounds of the people according to the number of the children of Israel" (Deuteronomy 32:8).

Referring to our time on this earth, the Prophet Joseph Smith was told: "Therefore, hold on thy way, and the priesthood shall remain with thee; for their [Joseph's enemies] bounds are set, they cannot pass. Thy days are known, and thy years shall not be numbered less; therefore, fear not what man can do, for God shall be with you forever and ever" (D&C 122:9).

President David O. McKay explained that the assignments of coming to this earth were made in accordance with our agency and willingness as well as our worthiness and preparation:

> By the operation of some eternal law with which man is yet unfamiliar, spirits come through parentages for which they are worthy—some as Bushmen of Australia, some as Solomon Islanders, some as Americans, as Europeans, as Asiatics, etc. etc., with all the varying degrees of mentality and spirituality manifest in parents of the different races that inhabit the earth. Of this we may be sure, each was satisfied and happy to come through the lineage to which he or she was attracted and for which, and only which, he or she was prepared.[22]

God's foreknowledge of all things, including the choices that we make on earth, does not impact our agency. Let us illustrate this with an experience that involved our three-year-old son, Little John. Shortly after his mother had topped off a German chocolate cake, she left the kitchen. Little John entered the kitchen just after his mother left. His eyes fixated on that cake. His father was observing this drama from a position on the couch. He knew that Little John was going to go over and put his fingers into that cake, which he did, to the great dismay of his mother. The father's foreknowledge of Little John's behavior had no impact on Little John's choice to put his

---

[22] Llewelyn R. McKay, *Home Memories of President David O. McKay* (Salt Lake City: Deseret Book, 1956), 226.

fingers into that cake. Needless to say, the mother was upset that the father didn't stop little John.

What Did We Agree to Do When We Were Called and Elected?

What were we called and elected to do? What does all of this mean as it relates to your life and my life? It means that our spirits were held back from the foundations of the world to come forth in this day and during this age to fulfill the missions that we agreed to in the premortal existence. We agreed:

1. To proclaim the gospel,
2. To help redeem the dead, and
3. To help one another become our highest and best selves. (See Ephesians 4:11–13.)

Not only were we called to come to the earth at this time, but we were sustained [elected] by millions of our kindred spirits who raised their hands and sustained us one by one. Regarding our premortal existence, President John Taylor said at a Relief Society woman's meeting:

> As thy spirit beheld the scenes transpiring there [in the premortal existence], thou grewest in intelligence, thou sawest worlds upon worlds organized and peopled with thy kindred spirits who took upon them tabernacles, died, were resurrected, and receive their exaltation on the redeemed worlds they once dwelt upon. Thou being willing and anxious to imitate them, waiting and desirous to obtain a body, a resurrection and exaltation also. . . .Thou longed, thou sighed and thou prayed to thy Father in heaven for the time to arrive when thou couldst come to this earth . . .
>
> At length the time arrived, and thou heard the voice of thy Father saying, go daughter to yonder lower world, and take upon thee a tabernacle, and work out thy probation with fear and trembling and rise to exaltation. But daughter, remember you go on this condition, that is, you are to forget all things you ever saw, or knew be transacted in the [premortal] spirit world . . . but you must go and become one of the most helpless of all beings that I have created, while in your infancy, subject to sickness, pain, tears, mourning, sorrow and death. But when truth shall touch

the cords of your heart they will vibrate; then intelligence will illuminate your mind, and shed its luster in your soul, and you shall begin to understand the things you once knew . . . you shall then begin to understand and know the object of your creation. Daughter, go, and be faithful as thou has been in thy first estate.[23]

It is of interest to note that when President Joseph Fielding Smith was asked if everyone chose their parents in the premortal world, he responded, "Yes, for those for whom it was necessary." We continue to ponder on the significance of that statement. Echoing the words of President David O. McKay,

Each was satisfied and happy to come through the lineage to which he or she was attracted and for which, and only which, he or she was prepared. We can be confident that all these decisions respected the agency of the individual and the love and perfect knowledge of a loving Heavenly Father.[24]

There is challenge and adversity in everyone's life. No one who lives beyond birth will escape this life without being the victim of abuse, being lied to, being cheated, being taken advantage of, and being exposed to physical, emotional, and spiritual trials. But however bad our life may be, none of us will descend to the level of suffering experienced by Jesus Christ. When Joseph Smith pleaded with the Lord about his adversities, tribulations, and perils among false brethren—about being victimized by robbers, having false accusations leveled against him, being separated from his wife and children, and being cast into prison with his enemies prowling around him like wolves for the blood of a lamb—he was told:

And if thou shouldst be cast into the pit, or into the hands of murderers, and the sentence of death passed upon thee; if thou be cast into the deep; if the billowing surge conspire against thee; if fierce winds become thine enemy; if the heavens gather blackness, and all the elements combine to hedge up the way; and above all, if the very jaws of hell

---
[23] N.B. Lundwall, *The Vision* (Salt Lake City: Bookcraft, 1946), 145–148.
[24] McKay, *Home Memories*.

shall gape open the mouth wide after thee, know thou, my
son, that all these things shall give thee experience, and shall
be for thy good.

The Son of Man hath descended below them all. Art
thou greater than he? (D&C 122:7–8)

The Lord also counseled,

Search diligently, pray always, and be believing, and all
things shall work together for your good, if ye walk uprightly
and remember the covenant wherewith ye have covenanted
one with another. (D&C 90:24)

The Importance of a Mortal Body

The importance of obtaining a mortal body surpasses our ability to truly appreciate it because everyone we know has a mortal body. The Prophet Joseph Smith taught, "We came to this earth that we might have a body. . . . The great principle of happiness consists in having a body. The devil has no body and herein is his punishment."[25] Cain, who became a son of perdition, will rule over Lucifer precisely because Cain received a mortal body and will resurrect, whereas Lucifer will remain as a spirit throughout all eternity (see Moses 5:23; 1 Corinthians 15:21-22).

We can be assured that our kind and loving Heavenly Father has the eternal best interest of each of His children and has provided a way for each of them to become their highest and finest selves. A child who dies under horrific circumstances may very well have understood the importance of obtaining a mortal body. It is also true that the same child understood that in God's plan of salvation and happiness, he would have the opportunity to learn all he needed to learn in the spirit world after death—and, if need be, during the Millennium. He also understood that he would receive every blessing of the new and everlasting covenant, including that of marriage, that would allow him to reach his highest potential.

Because of our mortal limitations and our lack of appreciation for God's love and God's motivation to bring to pass the immortality and eternal lives of His children, many have falsely assumed that God's toleration of man's inhumanity to man means that God doesn't care. They are wrong—

---

[25] *Teachings of the Prophet Joseph Smith*, 181.

profoundly wrong. It was never intended that this mortal life was God's whole plan. This inability to see the big picture from God's point of view is the reason Paul declared, "If in this life only we have hope in Christ, we are of all men most miserable" (1 Corinthians 15:19). He also said, "For now we see through a glass, darkly; but then face to face: now I know in part; but then shall I know even as also I am known" (1 Corinthians 13:12).

Eventually every knee will bow and every tongue confess that God is a god of love, justice, and mercy, and that "He doeth not anything save it be for the benefit of the world; for he loveth the world, . . . Wherefore, he commandeth none that they shall not partake of his salvation" (2 Nephi 26:24).

As mentioned, God's plan to help each of His children become their highest and best self included a premortal calling and election where we were assigned a time to come to this earth and were foreordained to specific missions—not only during our sojourn on earth, but in the spirit world and in the millennial realm. As members of The Church of Jesus Christ of Latter-day Saints, we have a three-fold mission and foreordination:

1. To proclaim the gospel of Jesus Christ;
2. To help in all aspects of redeeming our kindred dead by completing necessary research and temple work in their behalf; and
3. To serve one another through various callings in the Church and through service to our fellowmen.

If you could part the veil between you and your ancestors in the spirit world as well as those yet to be born through your lineage and you could see them praying for you, would it make a difference in your commitment to love and pray? What if that same veil were uncovered, and you could see millions of spirits raising their hands to elect and sustain you in proclaiming the gospel, redeeming the dead, and helping one another to become our best selves? Would that make a difference? It is our personal testimony that these things are true.

I'm Not Worthy

You may not feel that you are that important and that your weaknesses prohibit others who are depending upon you. You may also feel that you are not good enough or worthy. You and I—along with the brother of Jared, Alma, and King Benjamin—are among those who don't feel as worthy as we would like to feel. The brother of Jared prayed,

> Now behold, O Lord, and do not be angry with thy servant because of his weakness before thee; for we know that thou art holy and dwellest in the heavens, and that we are unworthy before thee; because of the fall our natures have become evil continually; nevertheless, O Lord, thou hast given us a commandment that we must call upon thee, that from thee we may receive according to our desires. (Ether 3:2)

Alma counseled his son Shiblon to pray by saying, "O Lord, forgive my unworthiness, and remember my brethren in mercy—yea, acknowledge your unworthiness before God at all times" (Alma 38:14). Alma said of himself, "I am unworthy to glory of myself" (Mosiah 23:11).

While John was in prison on the Isle of Patmos, he received a great vision. The issue was who would be worthy to carry out the great Atonement and to open up the seven seals that represented man's time on earth:

> And I saw a strong angel proclaiming with a loud voice, Who is worthy to open the book, and to loose the seals thereof?
>
> And no man in heaven, nor in earth, neither under the earth, was able to open the book, neither to look thereon.
>
> And I wept much, because no man was found worthy to open and to read the book, neither to look thereon.
>
> And one of the elders saith unto me, Weep not: behold, the Lion of the tribe of Juda, the Root of David, hath prevailed to open the book, and to loose the seven seals thereof: . . .
>
> And they sung a new song, saying, Thou art worthy to take the book, and to open the seals thereof. . . .
>
> And I beheld, and I heard the voice of many angels round about the throne and the beast and the elders: and the number of them was ten thousand times ten thousand, and thousands of thousands;
>
> Saying with a loud voice, Worthy is the Lamb. . . . (Revelation 5:2–5, 9, 11–12)

Many years ago, John was in a summer class at BYU taught by Elder Bruce R. McConkie. The issue of worthiness came up. Elder McConkie said there were two states of being worthy. One involved being worthy as Jesus Christ was worthy. He made clear that none of us, as mortals, would ever be as worthy as Jesus Christ. The second state of worthiness involved answering correctly the temple recommend questions. He went on to point out that even when we are worthy of a temple recommend, we are far from perfect, and perfection is reserved for resurrected beings. He observed that Jesus did not claim perfection for Himself until He was resurrected (see 3 Nephi 12:48).

The prophet Micah asked about being worthy before the Lord:

> Wherewith shall I come before the Lord, and bow myself before the high God? shall I come before him with burnt offerings, with calves of a year old?
>
> Will the Lord be pleased with thousands of rams, or with ten thousands of rivers of oil? shall I give my firstborn for my transgression, the fruit of my body for the sin of my soul?
>
> He hath shewed thee, O man, what is good; and what doth the Lord require of thee, but to do justly, and to love mercy, and to walk humbly with thy God? (Micah 6:6–8)

To be acceptable to the Lord requires humility and willingness. The resurrected Lord told the survivors of the great disasters in the New World, "And ye shall offer for a sacrifice unto me a broken heart and a contrite spirit" (3 Nephi 9:20).

If we want the Lord to divinely intervene in the lives of our loved ones, we must demonstrate humility, diligence, and the prayer of faith. Willingness is evidence of our trust in the Lord. Is there anyone who cannot meet that standard of humility, diligence, and prayer?

Diligence means consistent and persistent effort. It means getting up one more time after being knocked down. It doesn't mean that we will never fall or falter. The Lord knew that we would make foolish and unwise choices and that we would sin. He also knew that we would grow line upon line and step by step.

Despite our feelings of inadequacy, our shortcomings, and even our poor choices and sins, we can repent and start over again and again until with the help of the Lord we prevail. President Russell M Nelson pointed out the need for "daily repentance":

> Whether you are diligently moving along the covenant path, have slipped or stepped from the covenant path, or can't even see the path from where you are now, I plead with you to repent. Experience the strengthening power of daily repentance—of doing and being a little better each day. When we choose to repent, we choose to change! We

allow the Savior to transform us into the best version of ourselves.[26]

The Lord does not want us to wait until we are nearly perfect before He uses us as instruments in His hands. It was acknowledged by the Lord that we are the "weak things of the world." As the weak, we "shall come forth and break down the mighty and strong . . . That the fulness of my gospel might be proclaimed by the weak and the simple unto the ends of the world, and before kings and rulers" (D&C 1:19, 23).

There is one redeeming characteristic that you and I possess that the Lord wants us to display even now in our imperfect state. It is our ability to love. In God's plan it was never about being perfect in mortality. There are things that God cares about and some things that don't matter (see D&C 61:22). God does not care about status in the world. He doesn't care if you are an Apostle or a recovering alcoholic. He cares about loving one another even as Christ has loved us. God and the thousands of souls that continue to sustain our mortal mission are looking for you and me to be men and women of love to those in our sphere of influence, however great or small that may be. Paul's declaration to the Ephesians pointed out that some are given to be Apostles and some are given to be [ministering] teachers, "For the perfecting of the saints, for the work of the ministry, for the edifying of the body of Christ" (Ephesians 4:12).

If I Were Lucifer

If I were Lucifer, I would do everything in my power to keep you from being a loving person. I would want you to complain and murmur about how unfair things are. I would want you to be frustrated about everything and so worried and preoccupied that you would be unable to love. I would turn you into a critic and fill your life with contention. I would want you to be depressed, discouraged, and overwhelmed with problems. I would wish that you would be angry with the Lord and not pray nor be active in the Church. I would want you to be desperate and hopeless. Above all, I would want you so distracted that you would feel unable to use your gift of loving those in your sphere of influence.

Now is the time to love. Our calling and election to love is a premortal doctrine that has already taken place. Now is the time for making our calling and election sure, here in mortality. This is the context in which we can

---
[26] "We Can Do Better and Be Better," *Ensign*, May 2019.

understand Peter's statement, "brethren, give diligence to make your calling and election sure: for if ye do these things, ye shall never fall" (see 2 Peter 1:4-10). Peter had reference to becoming "partakers of the divine nature" and to acquiring "charity," which is the pure love of Christ (see Moroni 7:47).

Calling and election has already happened. The "calls" were extended and accepted in the premortal Council in Heaven. The "election" or sustaining votes have been counted and those of us on earth have already been elected to love. We have all been foreordained, "called and elected." Now is the day of our probation. Now is the time for us to perform our premortal callings with love. As stated by Alma, "And thus we see, that there was a time granted unto man to repent, yea, a probationary time, a time to repent and serve God" (Alma 42:4). Few are called to be prophets and Apostles. Most of us were called to be parents, ministering teachers, or regular members of the Church. Single, married, or divorced, it doesn't matter. What does matter is that we learn from our poor choices, repent of our sins, and focus on loving those within our sphere of influence now.

Recommitting oneself to one's premortal and foreordained mission to learn and apply love here on earth can happen at eighteen or eighty, as long as the breath of life remains. Obviously, the sooner the better. Most of us can look back with regrets over wasted time and lost opportunities. However, it is not too late to love and have faith and hope in what Jesus said in defense of Mary, who washed the Savior's feet with her tears and dried them with the hairs of her head and anointed him with spikenard. Jesus said of her, "Her sins, which are many, are forgiven; for she loved much" (Luke 7:47) . . . and "she hath done what she could" (Mark 14:8).

Not even one soul lacks the capacity to love and do what he or she can do, even under adverse circumstances. We all have our excuses, rationalizations, and justifications. The real question becomes one of *willingness* to love and not the *ability* to love. President Thomas S. Monson encouraged members to re-evaluate their lives.

> I have found that, rather than dwelling on a negative, if we will take a step back and consider the blessings in our lives, including seemingly small, sometimes overlooked blessings, we can find greater happiness. . . .
>
> I testify that much of that joy comes as we recognize that we can communicate with our Heavenly

Father through prayer and those prayers will be heard and answered—perhaps not how and when we expected they would be answered, but they *will* be answered and by a Heavenly Father who knows and loves us perfectly and who desires our happiness. Hasn't He promised us, "Be thou humble, and the Lord thy God shall lead thee by the hand, and give thee answer to thy prayers"?[27]

Mary and Her Unforgiving Daughter-in-Law

It was difficult for Mary to have children. She married at thirty-four years of age. After trying for three years to get pregnant, she and her husband, Fred, went to a fertility clinic and underwent extensive testing. The doctors concluded that Mary's ovaries were malfunctioning and recommended in vitro fertilization (IVF) or adoption. The cost for IVF was in excess of $10,000 per operation with no guarantee of success. Nevertheless, pregnancy resulted after the second attempt and produced a healthy baby boy. They named him Johnny, after Fred's father, John.

Fred was a plumber and worked hard to pay off the medical debt. This allowed Mary to quit her job and to stay home to care for little Johnny. Mary was a very responsible mother. Fred thought she was a little overprotective. She had a hard time letting Johnny sleep over at his friend's home, which was only two houses away. Later, when Johnny was in high school, she was reluctant to let him play football for fear that he would be injured.

Fred had served an LDS mission to Canada, and both Fred and Mary were active members of the Church. They prayed together every morning and night, held weekly family home evenings, and Johnny attended seminary. In spite of her fears, Mary acquiesced to let Johnny be active in sports, and he was elected captain of the football team. He didn't qualify for an athletic scholarship for college, but his grades were good enough for a partial scholarship that paid for tuition and books during his freshman year.

Johnny was pleasant and outgoing and had a number of friends. When he was nineteen, Johnny was called to serve a mission in Brazil. He was a good missionary, and his last assignment was as a zone leader in Rio de Janeiro. Johnny was home from his mission for only a couple of weeks before he was off to college.

---

27 "Consider the Blessings," *Ensign*, November 2012.

It was a difficult transition for Mary. She had dedicated her entire life to Johnny. She wanted him to live at home and attend a local college. Johnny had other plans and was determined to attend the university where he could become an architect. Johnny came home for Thanksgiving and Christmas, but not for spring break. He had been dating several girls but was most attracted to Sue, who was from a small town in Alabama. During spring break, Johnny went to Alabama to meet Sue's parents. The next weekend Johnny asked his parents to meet Sue, and Johnny announced his engagement to be married. Mary was shocked and somewhat cautious and reserved around Sue. Mary thought that Sue was a little demanding and selfish. Though Mary didn't express her reservations to anyone other than Fred, Sue could feel her future mother-in-law's subdued attitude.

As time went on, the relationship between Sue and Mary became strained. Sue continued to be demanding and selfish but Johnny didn't mind. Mary did. Eventually there was an exchange of harsh words between Mary and Sue. As a result, Johnny came to visit his parents without Sue. Things got even worse: after the birth of their son, Thomas, Sue was unwilling to let Mary see her only grandchild.

It was then that I got involved when Fred and Mary came to me for counseling. They were both upset and frustrated, especially Mary. Knowing that they were both faithful members of the Church, I was able to address a spiritual solution. Mary did not feel that she had done anything wrong and that Sue was just being selfish and punitive in not allowing her to see her only grandchild. I asked Mary, in particular, what she wanted as a favorable outcome. Mary said she wanted to see her grandson.

"If seeing your grandson is your objective, are you willing to reconcile with Sue?" I explained to Mary that Sue was obviously aware of her mother-in-law's non-acceptance. In response, Mary gave me numerous examples of Sue's selfish nature in relation to her son, Johnny.

In the kindest way possible, I told Mary that Johnny's relationship with Sue was really none of her business. Johnny loved Sue and was willing to tolerate her selfishness. What Mary needed to do was to write a letter to Sue and apologize for not being more accepting of her. I asked Mary to take her love to Sue and her frustrations about Sue to the Lord. She was not to complain to Fred or her sisters or to anyone else about her selfish daughter-in-law. Mary's job was to appreciate the good in Sue, to show acceptance and even affection for the woman her son had chosen to marry.

The solution I proposed was indeed a spiritual one that dealt with forgiveness and acceptance. I asked Mary to make a list of the good traits she saw in Sue—good characteristics that others could also see in Sue. Mary was to include one or two of those characteristics in the letter in which she apologized to Sue and asked Sue for her forgiveness.

I told Mary that I wanted to see the letter before she sent it. During that week, she and Fred were to pray that the Lord would soften Sue's heart and allow them to see their grandchild.

I had to make a major correction in half of the letter Mary wanted to send to Sue. Mary tried to explain in the letter why she reacted the way she did. I told Mary that it didn't matter why she did what she did or why she said what she said. Her explanations came across as justification, meaning that Mary really wasn't at fault after all. When giving an apology or when asking for forgiveness, you should never try to explain your behavior. The only thing acceptable to Sue would be for Mary to apologize for her harsh words.

Sue may have been equally responsible for the unkind words they exchanged. So I said to Mary, "Do you want to be right in your own mind or do you want to see your grandson?" She wanted to see her grandson. I told both Fred and Mary that they would have to be humble, patient, and exercise the prayer of faith. Mary was correct in her observation that Sue was selfish, but it was not up to Mary to be a judge. As a disciple of Jesus Christ, it was Mary's responsibility to love and forgive. Mary was not called to judge; she was called to love. It would be the Lord's responsibility to soften Sue's heart.

For an entire month, Fred and Mary heard nothing from either Johnny or Sue. Johnny was in the awkward position of choosing between his wife and his mother. It was difficult but appropriate that Johnny chose to sustain his wife. As the scriptures teach, "Therefore shall a man leave his father and his mother and shall cleave unto his wife" (Genesis 2:24). It was painful for Mary to hear that, but she accepted it.

After a month, Johnny called and asked Mary if she would be okay if he brought Thomas for a visit. Sue would not be coming. Johnny and Thomas could stay for only one day, and then they would have to return home. Mary and Fred were ecstatic but disappointed that Sue did not come.

Mary's prayer was answered, and Sue's heart was sufficiently softened to allow Mary and Fred to see their only grandchild. But the story doesn't end here. Over the next couple of years, Mary got rid of her pride. She made multiple efforts to extend an olive branch to Sue. Finally, Sue and Mary met at Thomas's fourth birthday party. Sue was cautious, but Mary was gracious and made every effort to make Sue feel accepted and appreciated. Sue was still selfish and demanding, but somehow that didn't matter to Mary anymore.

Eventually Sue came to trust her mother-in-law, and they actually became friends. None of this would have happened had Mary and Fred not been humble, diligent, and exercised the prayer of faith. They took their love to Sue—meaning they extended to Sue their acceptance, appreciation, and affection. They took their frustrations about Sue to the Lord.

During the period of time that Sue would not interact with Mary, something very important happened. When Mary's sisters and friends asked her about her relationship with Sue, Mary was not critical of Sue. Mary maintained a positive attitude and pointed out that things were improving. It would have been easy for Mary to seek sympathy from her sisters and friends. She could have played the martyr's role and sought for victimhood. But had she done so, her negative comments would have eventually reached Sue, and Mary would have come across as two-faced (one who speaks one thing to your face and another behind your back).

"Yea, speak no ill" is still the best course for Mary. Sue will probably die a demanding and selfish woman. But Mary will die having had a wonderful relationship with her daughter-in-law and with her only grandchild, Thomas.

Making Your Calling and Election Sure

Mary may also die having learned to love much and do what she could do. As she and Fred endure to the end of their mortal lives as faithful members of the Church, they may find their callings and elections were made sure.

Some may have to wait to have their calling and election made sure in the spirit world or during the Millennium. But there is a way to have your calling and election made sure in this life. Faithfully fulfilling one's premortal and foreordained mission here on earth is one way, and that is accomplished through valiant and loving service in this life. This can be loving service as a wife, mother, and disciple of Christ. The Lord has authorized three known ways for a person to be "sealed up unto eternal life."

The First Way

The first way for a person to be "sealed up" is through direct communication from the Lord. The Prophet Joseph taught:

> When the Lord has thoroughly proved him, and finds that the man is determined to serve Him at all hazards, then the man will find his Calling and Election made sure, then it will be his privilege to receive the other Comforter

[Jesus as found in John 14:18], which the Lord promised the Saints.[28]

Three examples of where the Lord directly sealed someone up are recorded in the scriptures in the stories of Joseph Smith, Alma, and Nephi, the son of Helaman.

1. Speaking to Joseph Smith, the Lord said: "For I am the Lord thy God, and will be with thee even unto the end of the world, and through all eternity; for verily I seal upon you your exaltation, and prepare a throne for you in the kingdom of my Father, with Abraham your father. Behold, I have seen your sacrifices, and will forgive all your sins; . . . as I accepted the offering of Abraham of his son Isaac" (D&C 132:49–50).
2. Speaking to Alma, the Lord said: "Thou art my servant; and I covenant with thee that thou shalt have eternal life; and thou shalt serve me and go forth in my name, and shalt gather together my sheep" (Mosiah 26:20).
3. Speaking to Nephi, the son of Helaman, the Lord said: "Blessed art thou, Nephi, for those things which thou hast done; for I have beheld how thou hast with unwearyingness declared the word, which I have given unto thee, unto this people. And thou hast not feared them, and hast not sought thine own life, but hast sought my will, and to keep my commandments. And now, because thou hast done this with such unwearyingness, behold, I will bless thee forever" (Helaman 10:4–5).

All of these appearances of the Savior are consistent with the promises of the Lord given in the scriptures (see D&C 67:10; 76:116–117; 88:68; 101:38; 110:1–2). This experience is also available to "every soul who forsaketh his sins and cometh unto me, and calleth on my name, and obeyeth my voice, and keepeth my commandments," for those who do so "shall see my face and know that I am" (D&C 93:1). Having this direct communication would be extremely comforting. However, it is not a necessary earthy experience. There are other times when one's calling and election can be made sure.

---

[28] *Teachings of the Prophet Joseph Smith*, 150.

The Second Way

The second way to have one's calling and election made sure is to be "sealed up" by the prophet, also known as the "more sure word of prophecy."

When the Lord took Peter, James, and John to Caesarea Philippi, the Lord informed Peter that he would be given the keys of the kingdom of heaven and that "whatsoever thou shalt bind on earth shall be bound in heaven: and whatsoever thou shalt loose on earth shall be loosed in heaven" (Matthew 16:19).

That authority was restored to the Prophet Joseph Smith: "Therefore, the keys of this dispensation are committed into your hands" (D&C 110:16). "The more sure word of prophecy means a man's knowing that he is sealed up unto eternal life, by revelation and the spirit of prophecy, through the power of the Holy Priesthood" (D&C 131:5).

Similar to the process used in issuing a recommend for a patriarchal blessing, early Latter-day Saints were interviewed by their stake president and recommended to the prophet of the Lord to receive what is called "the second anointing." This was also called the "second endowment" or the "more sure word of prophecy," which is tantamount to having one's calling and election made sure.

The recommend process for receiving one's "second anointing" was changed by President Joseph F. Smith sometime between 1902 and 1904. Under President Smith, the responsibility for recommending people for their "second anointing" was transferred to a responsible few, which is how it remains today.

It is very important to understand that one does not seek the experience of the "second anointing"; instead, one is recommended by a General Authority. Generally, such an invitation is extended after a lifetime of devoted service to building up the kingdom of God. Most important, a revelation is given to the prophet in each individual circumstance. It would be inappropriate to ever approach the prophet or any General Authority and even ask about the "second anointing." Such a process is sacred and based on revelation.

While John was serving in a stake presidency in Logan, Utah, the Logan Temple was under reconstruction. A construction worker who was in his stake discovered a stack of second anointing recommends dated in the late 1890s and early 1900s lodged between the inner and outer wall of the temple. When he brought them to John, John recognized what they were and immediately turned them over to the office of the First Presidency. Journals of some of the early Saints also disclosed some of this information. The most important point to remember is the sacred nature of this ordinance.

The Third Way

The third way to have one's calling and election made sure is to endure to the end of one's mortal life. Numerous scriptures as well as teachings of living and past prophets relate to this promise. King Benjamin stated,

> I say unto you, if ye have come to a knowledge of the goodness of God, and his matchless power, and his wisdom, and his patience, and his long-suffering towards the children of men; and also, the atonement which has been prepared from the foundation of the world, that thereby salvation might come to him that should put his trust in the Lord, and should be diligent in keeping his commandments, and continue in the faith even unto the end of his life, I mean the life of the mortal body—
>
> I say, that this is the man who receiveth salvation, through the atonement which was prepared from the foundation of the world for all mankind, which ever were since the fall of Adam, or who are, or who ever shall be, even unto the end of the world. (Mosiah 4:6–7)

Nephi bore his testimony:

> And I heard a voice from the Father, saying: Yea, the words of my Beloved are true and faithful. He that endureth to the end, the same shall be saved.
>
> And now, my beloved brethren, I know by this that unless a man shall endure to the end, in following the example of the Son of the living God, he cannot be saved. (2 Nephi 31:15–16)

In a discourse about the salvation of children, Elder Bruce R. McConkie made clear that in the scriptures, to be *exalted* and to be *saved* were synonymous terms:

> Eternal life is life in the highest heaven of the celestial world; it is exaltation; it is the same kind of life God lives. It consists of a continuation of the family unit in eternity. We have quoted scripture saying that children will be saved in the celestial kingdom, but now face the further query as to whether this includes the greatest of all the gifts of God—

the gift of eternal life. And in the providences of Him who is infinitely wise the answer is in the affirmative. Salvation means eternal life; the two terms are synonymous; they mean exactly the same thing. Joseph Smith said, "Salvation consists in the glory, authority, majesty, power and dominion which Jehovah possesses and in nothing else." (*Lectures on Faith* pp. 63–67.) We have come to speak of this salvation as exaltation—which it is—but all of the scriptures in all of the standard works call it salvation. I know of only three passages in all our scriptures which use salvation to mean something other and less than exaltation.[29]

In the following scripture, to *be saved* means to be exalted in the celestial kingdom of God. This is underscored in Nephi's discourse:

> Wherefore, ye must press forward with a steadfastness in Christ, having a perfect brightness of hope, and a love of God and of all men. Wherefore, if ye shall press forward, feasting upon the word of Christ, and endure to the end, behold, thus saith the Father: Ye shall have eternal life. (2 Nephi 31:20)

Eternal life is the kind of life that God the Father lives. It should bring great peace to all Latter-day Saints to know that the premortal calling and election can be assured by loving and faithfully serving to build up the kingdom of God on earth and doing so until they die. The vast majority of faithful members of the Church will have their calling and election made sure by enduring to the end of their mortal lives, as mentioned by King Benjamin (see Mosiah 4:6–7).

Regardless of when one's calling and election occurs, children will be eternally bound to their parents because of the special promise extended as part of that process. The Prophet Joseph Smith testified that having the calling and election made sure binds the Lord to a promise and a covenant: "When a seal is put upon the father and mother, it secures their posterity, so that they cannot be lost, but will be saved by virtue of the covenant of the father and mother."[30]

In quoting the Prophet, Orson F. Whitney taught:

---

[29] "The Salvation of Little Children," *Ensign*, April 1977.
[30] "Faithful Parents and Wayward Children," *Ensign*, March 2014.

The Prophet Joseph Smith declared—and he never taught a more comforting doctrine—that the eternal sealings of faithful parents and the divine promises made to them *for valiant service in the Cause of Truth*, would save not only themselves, but likewise their posterity.³¹

The doctrine of being "called and elected" happened in the premortal world, and the process of "making it sure" in mortality is within the grasp of every soul.

All of us can dedicate and rededicate ourselves to be more loving, "for valiant service in the cause of truth." It should bring peace, hope, and encouragement to all of us to know that faithfully enduring to the end of our mortal lives can bring all of the promised blessings.

Be Wary of Perfectionism

At a stake conference in Logan, Utah, on March 14, 1982, Elder McConkie said that too many Latter-day Saints form a standard of perfection for themselves greater than that which the Lord requires. The Lord's standard is to be worthy of—or on the path to becoming worthy of—a temple recommend and to endure to the end of our mortal life worthy of that recommend. Early in June 1980, Elder McConkie gave a discourse at BYU on "The Seven Deadly Heresies," in which he stated that the seventh deadly heresy was perfectionism in this life. In that same discourse, he said:

> Good and faithful members of the church will be saved, even though they are far from perfect in this life...If men had to be perfect and live all of the law strictly, wholly, and completely, there would be only one saved person in eternity [Jesus Christ]. The prophet [Joseph Smith] taught that there are many things to be done, even beyond the grave, in working out our salvation.

In a later address given at the University of Utah, Elder McConkie spoke in the plainest terms:

> This is a true gospel verity—that everyone in the Church who is on the straight and narrow path, who is

---

³¹ See Conference Report, April 1929, 110; emphasis added.

> striving and struggling and desiring to do what is right, though is far from perfect in this life; if he passes out of this life while he is on the straight and narrow, he's going to go on to eternal reward in his Father's kingdom.
>
> We don't need to get a complex or get a feeling that you have to be perfect to be saved. You don't. . . .
>
> You don't have to . . . "Go beyond the mark [Jacob 4:14]." You don't have to live a life that's truer than true. You don't have to have an excessive zeal that becomes fanatical and becomes unbalancing. What you have to do is stay in the mainstream of the Church and live as upright and decent people live in the Church—keeping the commandments, paying your tithing, serving in the organizations of the Church, loving the Lord, staying on the straight and narrow path. If you are on that path when death comes—because this is the time and the day appointed, this the probationary estate—you'll never fall off from it, and for all practical purposes, your calling and election is made sure.[32]

Two other talks given in the general conferences of the Church—one by President Russell M. Nelson on "Perfection Pending," and another by Elder Jeffery R. Holland titled "Be Ye Therefore Perfect—Eventually"—deal with this issue of members of the Church feeling inadequate and not good enough. If we can repent, love, and be on the pathway to developing a Christlike character, then we can trust a kind and loving Father in Heaven to give us the experiences we will need to return to Him.

As we seek to overcome the adversities we have already faced and will yet have to face, we can have confidence that as we remain humble and prayerful the Lord will sustain us and strengthen us. With prayer we are never alone.

> There hath no temptation taken you but such as is common to man: but God is faithful, who will not suffer you to be tempted above that ye are able; but will with the temptation also make a way to escape, that ye may be able to bear it. (1 Corinthians 10:13)

---

[32] "The Probationary Test of Mortality," address given at University of Utah, January 10, 1982.

How Has the Lord Prepared Us For Life on Earth?

In our attempts and best efforts to love those in our sphere of influence, the Lord has given every child of God an internal compass that we refer to as a conscience or the Light of Christ (see D&C 88:7–13). When you have occasion to question whether you should do something, you might notice an inner voice warning you not to do it. When a store clerk errs in giving you a ten-dollar bill instead of a one-dollar bill in change, your conscience will prompt you to give it back. That is the Light of Christ. It can grow and become brighter as you do "good things" like studying the scriptures, praying with a sincere heart, visiting the sick, and other loving behaviors (see D&C 93:28). Sadly, we can dim the Light of Christ by ignoring the promptings of our conscience and by believing false traditions of our fathers, such as believing that there is such a thing as constructive criticism (see D&C 93:39). To construct is to build; to criticize is to tear down. They involve two different and opposite behaviors. It is a false tradition that both can be accomplished at the same time.

In addition to the Light of Christ, our Heavenly Father assigned the Holy Ghost to bear witness to your soul and mine the truth of all things. Whether it's reading the Book of Mormon or discovering truth in a scientific laboratory, God will "manifest the truth of it unto you, by the power of the Holy Ghost. And by the power of the Holy Ghost ye may know the truth of all things" (Moroni 10:4–5).

We do not remember our premortal existence; the veil of forgetfulness was necessary for us to be fully tested and to learn to walk by faith in Christ during mortality. However, our kind and loving Heavenly Father has given each of us a conscience and multiple witnesses of the Holy Ghost, regardless of the circumstances under which we were born. If we will be true to ourselves and follow the inner compass, it will eventually lead us to faith in Christ. Whether it happens during mortality, during the spirit world, or during the Millennium, every knee will eventually bend and every tongue will confess that Jesus is the Christ (see Isaiah 45:23; Romans 14:11; Mosiah 27:31; D&C 76:110; D&C 88:104). Why? Because all souls will be exposed to Jesus, whom they sustained to be their Savior in the premortal Grand Council in heaven.

The Light of Christ and the Holy Ghost will bear witness that Jesus is our Savior. For some, that happens in a Primary class as a young child. For others, it happens when missionaries knock on the door and the individual is introduced to the gospel of Jesus Christ. For still others, it happens while reading the Book of Mormon or kneeling in prayer.

Once such witness is borne, it becomes the responsibility of the individual to nourish that testimony through study and prayer. Failure to do so will result in doubt replacing faith in Christ.

Faith in Christ is generally followed by repentance. The most common Hebrew word for repentance is *nacham*; it means to "sigh or breathe strongly in sorrow." Another Hebrew word used for repentance is *shuwb*, which means "to turn away." The Greek words for repentance—*metanoeo* and *metanoia*—mean to "think differently" and "reform."

True repentance involves sorrow for poor choices and for the hurt, the heartache, and the sorrow we may have caused others. It also requires that we think differently about our behavior. Just stopping bad behavior without changing our thinking is not repentance.

For those who exercise faith in Christ, the time will come when they will have the opportunity to be baptized. That may happen in mortality, or one may have their baptism performed vicariously after they are dead in one of the temples of the Lord.

After baptism, one is authorized to enjoy the companionship of the Holy Ghost. The difference between a witness of the Holy Ghost and the companionship of the Holy Ghost is significant. A *witness of the Holy Ghost* occurs for everyone who encounters a truth. The *companionship of the Holy Ghost* means that the Holy Ghost may accompany the individual wherever he or she goes. Imagine going to a library and finding a book titled *Truth*. Now imagine leaving the library and taking with you a memory about that book. That is equivalent to a witness of the Holy Ghost. Being able to take the book with you is akin to having the companionship of the Holy Ghost.

Faith in Christ followed by repentance and baptism leads to the challenge of learning to live with the Holy Ghost without offending Him. This is often a lifelong process. Why? Because we keep learning of behaviors we need to change. The process of learning to live with the Holy Ghost is called *sanctification*. As we learn to change our thinking and adjust our behaviors to conform to the companionship of the Holy Ghost, we are literally repenting from week to week. That process underscores the importance of weekly partaking of the sacrament to renew all the covenants we have made to become disciples of the Lord Jesus Christ.

We live in a telestial world filled with both good and evil and with trials of every kind. As a result, we are constantly required to evaluate our choices. As we persist in making good choices, it becomes easier to follow Jesus. When we slip and fall, as we all do in spite of our best intentions, we can repent and return to the pathway that will lead us back to our Heavenly Father. Diligence and persistence in living with the Holy Ghost is called "enduring to the end."

We can all be true to ourselves and to our own conscience and be guided by the Light of Christ and witnesses of the Holy Ghost as we develop faith in Christ. We can repent, be baptized, and learn to live with the Holy Ghost. We can endure to the end of our mortal life, seeking to love and live with the Holy Ghost. We can seek to do one loving behavior every day. We can take our love to our loved ones and take our frustrations to the Lord. We can count our many blessings. We can rejoice in the fact that Jesus has prepared a way for our escape from physical and spiritual death. This is the gospel:

> And this is the gospel, the glad tidings, which the voice out of the heavens bore record unto us—
>
> That he came into the world, even Jesus, to be crucified for the world, and to bear the sins of the world, and to sanctify the world, and to cleanse it from all unrighteousness;
>
> That through him all might be saved whom the Father had put into his power and made by him;
>
> Who glorifies the Father, and saves all the works of his hands, except those sons of perdition who deny the Son after the Father has revealed him.
>
> Wherefore, he saves all except them.... (D&C 76:40–44)

Some will learn more quickly than others. Some will learn by observation; others will learn by trial and error; and some will only learn by the consequences of their poor choices. The Lord has said, "And my people must needs be chastened until they learn obedience, if it must needs be, by the things which they suffer" (D&C 105:6).

When you have a child or a loved one who is learning by the things he or she is suffering, it is difficult not to become a critic of those poor choices. In more than five decades of counseling, John has yet to find a wayward child or spouse who was unaware of disappointing a loved one. What most of them lacked was not knowledge of their poor choices. What they lacked was motivation to change in spite of disappointing their loved ones.

What Motivates Change?

People change from the inside out. Criticism is an external force that seldom changes anything for the good. (The single exception, of course, is appropriate criticism inspired by the Holy Ghost, which is rare.) Uninspired and inappropriately given criticism alienates, offends, and supports contention and destroys the motivation to even try.

Those who think that uninspired criticism changes behavior often confuse conformity with behavioral change. Conformity is often a mask for silent rebellion and passive-aggressive behavior. Conformity sustained by criticism creates the classic attitude, "When the cat's away, the mice will play." The one criticized did not actually change—he or she only acted the way the critic wanted in order to avoid conflict.

Research tells as that behavioral change is motivated by three main factors: fear, reward, and love.

Fear is an effective and sometimes necessary short-term motivator. But fear as a motivator is effective only for a short while. Keeping an individual, a family, or a nation in constant fear requires an incredible amount of consistent negative messaging. Fear may temporarily conform behavior but seldom changes behavior. For example, consider speeding in a car: a driver who sees or suspects that a policeman or camera is watching will conform by obeying the speed limit. But when fear of getting a ticket is removed, many drivers speed back up. Most of those who abide by the speed limit even while not being watched do it because they are motivated by something else, such as the satisfaction of knowing that they are abiding by the laws of the land.

Reward is a major motivator. Slot machines have proven that frequent intermittent rewards are the most effective at keeping people motivated. Because intermittent rewards are more productive motivators, John has recommended that employers estimate what they might give as a Christmas or year-end bonus and instead give their employees several intermittent smaller bonuses throughout the year.

There is an axiom in behavioral psychology: "Behavior rewarded is behavior repeated." Fixed rewards can be great motivators. Most of us understand the consistent reward of a paycheck. Even very young toddlers can learn to be potty-trained as they are consistently rewarded with M&M candies. Other kinds of rewards work well, too. For example, a restaurant manager posts a picture of an outstanding waitress on the bulletin board as recognition for exemplary service. Two months later, the manager gives the employee a fifty-dollar bill for being friendly and responsive to customers.

By far the greatest and most long-lasting motivator is love. It is helpful to define love using the four *A*'s: attraction, acceptance, affection, and appreciation.

When someone says, "I love you," they are usually saying they are attracted to you, they accept you, they feel affection for you, and/or they appreciate you.

This demonstrates why inappropriate and uninspired criticism is so counterproductive. Criticism sends a message of rejection, non-acceptance, lack of affection, and no appreciation. Even when inspired by the Holy Ghost, the giver of criticism is counseled to show forth an "increase of love toward him whom thou hast reproved, lest he esteem thee to be his enemy" (D&C 121:43).

The Lord's way is to confirm the worth of the individual by showing forth acceptance for the person and being able to separate the negative behavior from an appreciation for the soul of the person. A good example is that of Jesus dealing with the woman taken in adultery. When Jesus invited those without sin to first cast a stone at her, the accusers left, convicted by their own conscience:

> And they which heard it, being convicted by their own conscience, went out one by one, beginning at the eldest, even unto the last: and Jesus was left alone, and the woman standing in the midst.
> When Jesus had lifted up himself, and saw none but the woman, he said unto her, Woman, where are those thine accusers? hath no man condemned thee?
> She said, No man, Lord. And Jesus said unto her, Neither do I condemn thee; go, and sin no more. (John 8:9–11)

Several important elements in this story relate to doing things in the Lord's way. The first is that Jesus addressed her as "woman," which is the same title of respect that He used for His mother (see John 19:26). John R. Dummelow said that in Greek, the language in which the New Testament was written, the title of *woman* was a title of respect meaning my "lady." As soon as Jesus addressed the woman with that title, He communicated respect for her as a person. In response to His query, "hath no man condemned thee?" (see John 8:10), she responded, "No man, Lord" (John 8:11). The Lord sent a clear message of acceptance of her as a child of God by saying, "Neither do I condemn thee" (John 8:11). The Lord then separated the behavior of adultery from the woman's personal worth and made it an independent issue from her value as a daughter of God by telling her to "go, and sin no more" (John 8:11).

What was the outcome of the Lord treating her with respect, acceptance, and appreciation? She repented.

Our Heavenly Father is a God of truth for he cannot lie. So when the Lord gives a promise, one can be positively and absolutely sure that he will fulfill his promise. The Lord has said, "I, the Lord, am bound when ye do what I say; but when ye do not what I say, ye have no promise" (D&C 82:10).

If we will cease to find fault one with another, humble ourselves before the Lord, and with diligent prayer and faith in Christ take our love to our loved ones and take all our frustrations and concerns to the Lord, we can bind the Lord to a promise. The Lord will divinely intervene in the lives of our loved ones. In other words, the Lord will take the primary role of changing the heart and behavior of our loved ones as we become instruments of acceptance, affection, and appreciation in the lives of our loved ones.

From a pragmatic point of view, criticizing your loved ones doesn't work. Haven't you had enough of the hurt, heartache, and sorrow that results from a conflicted relationship? The silent treatment doesn't work. Uninspired criticism doesn't work. Even inspired criticism poorly given doesn't work. Screaming, yelling, crying, and pleading don't seem to change behavior for the good. In fact, these negative behaviors only widen the emotional gap between people.

How Do We Take Upon Ourselves the Yoke of Christ?

Why not come unto Christ and take His yoke upon you? Listen to these words of invitation from the Lord:

> Come unto me, all ye that labour and are heavy laden, and I will give you rest.
>
> Take my yoke upon you, and learn of me; for I am meek and lowly in heart: and ye shall find rest unto your souls.
>
> For my yoke is easy, and my burden is light. (Matthew 11:28–30)

Before we embark on what the Lord will do to divinely intervene in the life of your loved one, let's examine what the "yoke of the Lord" is. The Lord invited His imperfect followers to love one another as He has loved us. The yoke is to love. Jesus eloquently outlined how we were to love one another while He was in the upper room during the Last Supper.

"As I have loved you, that ye also love one another" is the yoke (John 13:34). He called it a new commandment. How is loving a new commandment? There is a great insight to gain in the statement made by Jesus: "A new commandment I give unto you, That ye love one another; as I have loved you, that ye also love one another. By this shall all men know that ye are my disciples, if ye have love one to another" (John 13:34–35).

How was loving a new commandment? Throughout the ministry of Jesus, He was asked, "Master, which is the great commandment in the law?" (Matthew 22:36). The Lord responded, quoting from Deuteronomy 6:5, "Thou shalt love the Lord thy God with all thy heart, and with all thy soul, and with all thy mind" (Matthew 22:37). Jesus quickly added that the second greatest commandment—as was given in Leviticus 19:18—was a similar one: "Thou shalt love thy neighbour as thyself" (Matthew 22:39). Jesus then declared, "On these two commandments hang all the law and the prophets" (Matthew 22:40). Later the Lord reiterated His "new commandment" when He said, "This is my commandment, That ye love one another, as I have loved you" (John 15:12).

Under the law of Moses, the commandment was to love your neighbor as yourself, but the *new* commandment under the Christ was to love one another as Jesus loved His disciples. There is a significant difference between loving your neighbor as yourself and loving as Jesus loved. Loving one's neighbor as mentioned in Deuteronomy involves the Hebrew word *ahab* and corresponds to the Greek word *philos*, which means deep brotherly affection.

There are several Greek words for *love*, and since the New Testament was written in Greek, it becomes important to understand which words were used in Greek and translated into English. There are three Greek words commonly used for love: *agapao* or *agape* is the highest and noblest form of love and is the word Jesus used in John 13:34. *Phileo* or *philos* is a deep affection akin to brotherly love. *Eros* is the third word used for love, and it describes romantic or physical love.

On the shores of the Sea of Galilee, the Savior asked Peter the first time, "Simon, son of Jonas, lovest [*agape*] thou me more than these [implying these fish, men, and things of this world]?" (John 21:15). In other words, "Peter, do you love me with the purest and noblest love, even as I have loved you?"

Peter answered; "Lord . . . thou knowest that I love [*philos*] thee" (John 21:15). In other words, "Yes, I love you as a brother."

At that point the Savior said in essence, "If you love me as a brother, feed my lambs "of me," meaning, "as I have loved you." *Of me* is not in the King James Version or most English translations, but it *is* in the original Greek New Testament. Jesus wasn't asking Peter to feed the hungry; He was asking Peter to spiritually feed His sheep the doctrine of this higher form of love—namely, charity.

The Lord asked Peter a second time, "Simon, son of Jonas, lovest [*agape*] thou me?" (John 21:16).

Once again, Peter answered Him, "Yea, Lord; thou knowest that I love [*philos*] thee," to which Jesus replied, "Feed my sheep" (John 21:17).

The Lord asked Peter yet a third time, but this time He used the word *philos* in asking about Peter's love. It grieved Peter that the Lord used the word *philos* rather than *agape*. The Lord was basically saying to Peter, "Even if you don't love me with the highest form of love (*agape*, or charity), and you love only with a deep, abiding, brotherly affection (*philos*), I want you to feed my sheep and teach them to love as I have loved you" (see John 21:18).

The English translators of the King James Version chose to translate both *agape* and *philos* with the English word *love*. But we must not forget that the "new commandment" is to love with *agape*—the highest form of love, or charity, which is also known as the pure love of Christ—as Jesus loved His disciples, and not to love with the lesser love of *philos*, the brotherly love described under the law of Moses.

The Ultimate Objective of Jesus Is to Teach Us to Love One Another as God Loves

Understanding the love of Jesus is defined as understanding the pure love of Christ. It is what the Apostle Paul defined as *charity*. How important is learning to love with the pure love of Christ as opposed to other spiritual gifts? The answer is that all other spiritual gifts pale in comparison:

> Though I speak with the tongues of men and of angels, and have not charity, I am become as sounding brass, or a tinkling cymbal.
> And though I have the gift of prophecy, and understand all mysteries, and all knowledge; and though I have all faith, so that I could remove mountains, and have not charity, I am nothing.
> And though I bestow all my goods to feed the poor, and though I give my body to be burned, and have not charity, it profiteth me nothing. (1 Corinthians 13:1–3)

After declaring that the ultimate objective is to love one another with the pure love of Christ, or charity, Paul defined charity:

> Charity suffereth long, and is kind; charity envieth not; charity vaunteth not itself, is not puffed up,

> Doth not behave itself unseemly, seeketh not her own, is not easily provoked, thinketh no evil;
> Rejoiceth not in iniquity, but rejoiceth in the truth;
> Beareth all things, believeth all things, hopeth all things, endureth all things.
> Charity never faileth: but whether there be prophecies, they shall fail; whether there be tongues, they shall cease; whether there be knowledge, it shall vanish away. (1 Corinthians 13:4–8)

To Paul's definition, Mormon adds:

> Wherefore, cleave unto charity, which is the greatest of all, for all things must fail—
> But charity is the pure love of Christ, and it endureth forever; and whoso is found possessed of it at the last day, it shall be well with him.
> Wherefore, my beloved brethren, pray unto the Father with all the energy of heart, that ye may be filled with this love, which he hath bestowed upon all who are true followers of his Son, Jesus Christ; that ye may become the sons of God; that when he shall appear we shall be like him, for we shall see him as he is; that we may have this hope; that we may be purified even as he is pure. Amen. (Moroni 7:46–48).

Notice that Mormon refers to charity as the pure love of Christ. The law of Christ is not *an eye for an eye* or even *do unto others as you would have others do unto you*. It is a higher law that requires the disciples of Jesus to conquer the natural man and to exercise meekness, patience, and long-suffering. It invites us as disciples to take our love to our loved ones and our frustrations to the Lord.

Most of us fall short of loving as Jesus loved. We may be a lot like Peter, who at one time was able to love only with *philos*. The important thing is that we strive to leave behind us the natural man and natural woman. Loving as Christ loved is our objective. However, that is a journey that lasts our entire mortal life and beyond. We can take comfort in the teachings of the Prophet Joseph Smith:

> When you climb up a ladder, you must begin at the bottom, and ascend step by step, until you arrive at the top; and so it is with the principles of the gospel—you must begin with the first, and go on until you learn all the

principles of exaltation. But it will be a great while after you have passed through the veil before you will have learned them. It is not all to be comprehended in this world; it will be a great work to learn our salvation and exaltation even beyond the grave.[33]

Fortunately, the Lord does not require that we have perfect charity in order to divinely intervene in the lives of our loved ones. He does require that we diligently approach Him in humility and with the prayer of faith in Christ.

---

[33] *Teachings of the Prophet Joseph Smith*, 348.

CHAPTER FOUR

FIVE PRINCIPLES OF DIVINE INTERVENTION

THE SCRIPTURES ARE FILLED WITH examples of the Lord divinely intervening in the lives of His children. There are five major principles of divine intervention:

1. The most common intervention is *softening of the heart*.[34]
2. The second principle of divine intervention is *strengthening* the petitioner and the loved one physically, emotionally, and spiritually.[35]
3. The third principle of divine intervention is *raising someone up to do what you cannot do*.[36]
4. The fourth principle of divine intervention is the *exodus* principle in which you or your loved one are removed or led away from a difficult circumstance.[37]
5. The fifth principle of divine intervention is *removing the problem*.[38]

Let's look at how each of those principles of divine intervention work.

---

[34] See 1 Nephi 7:5; 1 Nephi 18: 20; Mosiah 23:28–29; D&C 105:27.
[35] See Isaiah 12:2; 40:29; 1 Nephi 17:3; Mosiah 9:17; 10:10; 24:14; Alma 2:18, 28, 31; 14:26; 20:4; 31:38; 44:5; 56:56; 58:10; 3 Nephi 3:12; Words of Mormon 1:14; D&C 9:12.
[36] See Genesis 12:1–5 (Abraham); Genesis 45:7 (Joseph of old); Judges 6:7, 14 (Gideon); 1 Nephi 3:29; 2 Nephi 1:24; Mosiah 27:36; Alma 1:8 (Gideon of the Book of Mormon); Alma 17:11; 26:3; 27:11–17 (an Angel); 29:9; Moroni 7:37; D&C 1:17 (Joseph Smith); Moses 1:41 (Moses).
[37] See 1 Nephi 2:2, 17:26; 2 Nephi 5:5; Jacob 3:4; Omni 1:12; Mosiah 2:4, 7:33, 11:26, 29:20; Alma 36:27, 38:4, 44:3, 48:15, 56:47, 57:35; Ether 9:3.
[38] See Exodus 14:28; Isaiah 37:36; 1 Nephi 4:12; Alma 44:3.

The First Principle of Divine Intervention: Softening of the Heart

In both Hebrew and Greek, the heart was a source of thinking as well as feeling; in Proverbs, we are told, "For as he thinketh in his heart, so is he" (Proverbs 23:7). A *hard heart* is used to describe a stubborn or hardheaded person or someone who has hard feelings. The Lord can soften both.

It's important to realize that the Lord *softens* hearts; He never hardens them. One good example of that is found in the Prophet Joseph Smith's translation of the Bible, which points out that Pharaoh's heart was not hardened by the Lord.[39] It is clear that Pharaoh hardened his own heart against Moses and the Lord. In another scriptural example, the prophet Job declared, "For God maketh my heart soft" (Job 23:16).

We have already seen in the case of Mary and Bill and his parents how hearts were softened. It is amazing and comforting to see the frequency with which the Lord softens the hearts of His children. A review of selected scriptures reveals how often the Lord's hand is engaged in softening the hearts of His offspring.

Apparently, Nephi's heart was originally hardened toward his father's teachings. Nephi said,

> I did cry unto the Lord; and behold he did visit me, and did soften my heart that I did believe all the words which had been spoken by my father; wherefore, I did not rebel against him like unto my brothers. (1 Nephi 2:16)

Notice the relationship between Nephi's prayer and the Lord softening Nephi's heart. Later the Lord spoke to Nephi and said, "Blessed art thou, Nephi, because of thy faith, for thou hast sought me diligently, with lowliness of heart" (1 Nephi 2:19). Nephi's ability to be blessed by the Lord depended on the three important elements of the prayer of faith, diligence, and humility (lowliness of heart).

Too often, we tend to believe that we are not important enough to have the Lord divinely intervene in our daily lives; we must overcome that tendency. If we are humble and diligent and exercise the prayer of faith in Christ, we are good enough to have the Lord bless us as he blessed Nephi. The Lord is anxious to bless His children. The Lord is not the one who keeps Himself or His blessings of divine intervention from us. *We* are the ones who

---

[39] See Exodus 9:12, JST ("And Pharaoh hardened his heart"); 10:1, JST ("for he hath hardened his heart"); 10:20, JST ("But Pharaoh hardened his heart"); 11:10, JST ("And Pharaoh hardened his heart").

hinder the hand of the Lord in our lives by our lack of humility, our lack of faith in Christ, and our failure to diligently seek the Lord in prayer.

We need to recognize that we are talking about the goodness of the Lord, not about our own goodness. It is not about faith in ourselves. What matters is our faith in Jesus Christ. With that thought in mind, we can look at scriptures that provide a window into how God deals with His children. In those scriptures are many examples of how often the Lord divinely intervened and softened the hearts of His children. Let's examine a few of them.

In the Book of Mormon, King Limhi and his people had heavy burdens placed upon their backs and were treated as slaves by the Lamanites. After three unsuccessful attempts to throw off the yoke of bondage, and the tremendous loss of life that resulted, Limhi's people were left with a great number of widows.

> And they did humble themselves even in the depths of humility; and they did cry mightily to God; yea, even all the day long did they cry unto their God that he would deliver them out of their afflictions.
>
> And now the Lord was slow to hear their cry because of their iniquities; nevertheless the Lord did hear their cries, and began to soften the hearts of the Lamanites.... (Mosiah 21:14–15)

When Alma and his people were in the city of Helam, a fearsome, but lost, army of Lamanites approached them. Alma instructed his people to have faith in the Lord their God and He would deliver them. Once again we see the relationship between prayer and the Lord softening the hearts of the Lamanites:

> Therefore they hushed their fears, and began to cry unto the Lord that he would soften the hearts of the Lamanites, that they would spare them, and their wives, and their children.
>
> And it came to pass that the Lord did soften the hearts of the Lamanites. (Mosiah 23:28–29)

There are several examples in the scriptures of the Lord using others to soften a heart. When Nephi's brothers bound him with cords and intended to kill him, one of the daughters of Ishmael pleaded with Laman and Lemuel to release him. We are told that because of her petition, "they did soften their hearts; and they did cease striving to take away my life" (1 Nephi 7:19).

Fearing that his brother Esau might want to take revenge on him for obtaining the birthright, Jacob prayed to the Lord to be delivered from Esau. Jacob offered more than four hundred animals as gifts with the hope that they might soften the heart of Esau, which they apparently did (see Genesis 32:9–21).

After Lehi and his family were led into the wilderness, Nephi and his brethren were sent back to Jerusalem to invite Ishmael and his family to join them in their journey. It is difficult to imagine someone knocking on your door and inviting you and your family to permanently leave your home and embark on an uncertain journey. However, that is exactly what happened. Nephi reported,

> And it came to pass that the Lord did soften the heart of Ishmael, and also his household, insomuch that they took their journey with us down into the wilderness to the tent of our father. (1 Nephi 7:5)

When necessary, the Lord allows the consequences of sin—such as war, pestilence, and famine to soften the hearts of the wicked. Moses pleaded with Pharaoh to "let my people go" (Exodus 10:3); despite his pleading, it took ten plagues in Egypt before Pharaoh softened his heart. The same thing happened when, while crossing the ocean, Nephi was once again bound by Laman and Lemuel. Nephi reported,

> . . . my wife with her tears and prayers, and also my children, did not soften the hearts of my brethren that they would loose me.
> And there was nothing save it were the power of God, which threatened them with destruction, could soften their hearts; wherefore, when they saw that they were about to be swallowed up in the depths of the sea they repented of the thing which they had done, insomuch that they loosed me. (1 Nephi 18:19–20)

Jacob, the brother of Nephi, warned that the Gentiles would eventually afflict the remnant of the Nephites and Lamanites because of the great wickedness they had brought upon themselves by their secret works of darkness, murders, and abominations. Mormon said, "it is by the wicked that the wicked are punished" (Mormon 4:5). However, the Lord made a promise to those faithful parents that in time he would soften the hearts of the Gentiles and deliver the wayward seed:

> For I will fulfill my promises which I have made unto the children of men. . . .
>
> I will afflict thy seed by the hand of the Gentiles; nevertheless, I will soften the hearts of the Gentiles, that they shall be like unto a father to them; wherefore, the Gentiles shall be blessed and numbered among the house of Israel.
>
> Wherefore, I will consecrate this land unto thy seed, and them who shall be numbered among thy seed, forever, for the land of their inheritance. . . . (2 Nephi 10:17–19)

These scriptures confirm the Lord's willingness to soften hearts. The Savior is also willing to divinely intervene in other ways. The second principle of divine intervention is *strengthening*.

The Second Principle of Divine Intervention: Strengthening You and Your Loved One Physically, Emotionally, and Spiritually

Another tool in the Lord's arsenal of love is to divinely intervene by physically, emotionally, and spiritually strengthening those who are humble, diligent, and prayerful.

> Behold, God is my salvation; I will trust, and not be afraid: for the Lord Jehovah is my strength and my song; he also is become my salvation. (Isaiah 12:2)

> He giveth power to the faint; and to them that have no might he increaseth strength.
>
> But they that wait upon the Lord shall renew their strength; they shall mount up with wings as eagles; they shall run, and not be weary; and they shall walk, and not faint. (Isaiah 40:29, 31)

President Monson reiterated a story of the Lord physically strengthening a young man during World War II:

> A faithful member of the Church, John A. Larsen, served during World War II in the United States Coast Guard on the ship USS *Cambria*. During a battle in the Philippines, word came of an approaching squadron of bombers and kamikaze fighter planes. Orders were given for immediate evacuation. Since the USS *Cambria* was already gone, John

and three companions gathered their gear and hurried to the beach, hoping for a lift out to one of the departing ships. Fortunately, a landing craft picked them up and sped toward the last ship leaving the bay. The men on that departing ship, in an effort to evacuate as quickly as possible, were busy on deck and had time only to throw ropes to the four men that they might hopefully be able to climb to the deck.

John, with a heavy radio strapped to his back, found himself dangling at the end of a 40-foot (12 m) rope, at the side of a ship headed out to the open sea. He began pulling himself up, hand over hand, knowing that if he lost his grip, he would almost certainly perish. After climbing only a third of the way, he felt his arms burning with pain. He had become so weak that he felt he could no longer hold on.

With his strength depleted, as he grimly contemplated his fate, John silently cried unto God, telling Him that he had always kept the Word of Wisdom and had lived a clean life—and he now desperately needed the promised blessings.

John later said that as he finished his prayer, he felt a great surge of strength. He began climbing once again and fairly flew up the rope. When he reached the deck, his breathing was normal and not the least bit labored. The blessings of added health and stamina promised in the Word of Wisdom had been his. He gave thanks to his Heavenly Father then, and throughout the remainder of his life, for the answer to his desperate prayer for help.[40]

John was impressed as a young man by the stories of Samson's strength. On one occasion, Samson encountered a young lion and killed the beast with his bare hands (see Judges 14:5–6). Later Samson slew thirty Philistines (see Judges 14:19). Probably the most famous story of Samson involved Samson slaying a thousand Philistines with the jawbone of an ass at a place called Lehi (see Judges 15:14–16). All these stories have one thing in common: "The Spirit of the Lord came mightily upon him" (Judges 14:6; also see Judges 15:14).

Unfortunately, there were also some undesirable aspects of Samson's story. Samson foolishly told Delilah that God had promised that as long as his hair was long and uncut he would maintain his strength. Delilah had

---

[40] Thomas S. Monson, "Principles and Promises," *Ensign*, November 2016.

Samson's hair cut; the Philistines blinded him and forced him to push a millstone while in prison.

Samson's hair eventually grew back. When the Philistine leaders met to celebrate and to offer a sacrifice to their god Dagon, a fish-headed god, more than three thousand were gathered on the roof of a stadium while they made sport of Samson.

> And Samson called unto the Lord, and said, O Lord God, remember me, I pray thee, and strengthen me. . . .
>
> And Samson took hold of the two middle pillars upon which the house stood, and on which it was borne up, of the one with his right hand, and of the other with his left.
>
> And Samson said, Let me die with the Philistines. And he bowed himself with all his might; and the house fell upon the lords, and upon all the people that were therein. (Judges 16:28–30)

Samson had as many weaknesses as he did strengths. In spite of those weaknesses, the Lord was willing to bless Samson as he humbled himself and called on the Lord in prayer.

In the Book of Mormon, Nephi was bound by his brothers and left to be devoured by wild beasts. Nephi prayed: "O Lord, according to my faith which is in thee, wilt thou deliver me from the hands of my brethren; yea, even give me strength that I may burst these bands with which I am bound" (1 Nephi 7:17). In answer to his prayer, the bands were loosed from off his hands and feet.

You Are as Important as Any Person in the Scriptures

The scriptures bear testimony to God's divine intervention in the lives of others. The stories in the scriptures are a witness that encourages you to invite God into your life and the life of your loved one.

Who needs physical strength more than Jennifer, a mother with four boys under the age of ten? What about Mike, who is Jennifer's husband? Mike is a self-employed construction worker who often works ten-hour days. Does Mike need to be physically strengthened at times? A widow with arthritis, Kathy has to care for a granddaughter. Does Kathy need physical help?

It is often true that these very real people need emotional and spiritual strength as well as physical strength to survive the daily rigors of life. Help is available. Remember the Lord's plea: "How often would I have gathered thy children together, even as a hen gathereth her chickens under her wings, and ye would not!" (Matthew 23:37).

Elder Dieter F. Uchtdorf related the following story:

> There once was a man whose lifelong dream was to board a cruise ship and sail the Mediterranean Sea. He dreamed of walking the streets of Rome, Athens, and Istanbul. He saved every penny until he had enough for his passage. Since money was tight, he brought an extra suitcase filled with cans of beans, boxes of crackers, and bags of powdered lemonade, and that is what he lived on every day.
>
> He would have loved to take part in the many activities offered on the ship—working out in the gym, playing miniature golf, and swimming in the pool. He envied those who went to movies, shows, and cultural presentations. And, oh, how he yearned for only a taste of the amazing food he saw on the ship—every meal appeared to be a feast! But the man wanted to spend so very little money that he didn't participate in any of these. He was able to see the cities he had longed to visit, but for the most part of the journey, he stayed in his cabin and ate only his humble food.
>
> On the last day of the cruise, a crew member asked him which of the farewell parties he would be attending. It was then that the man learned that not only the farewell party but almost everything on board the cruise ship—the food, the entertainment, all the activities—had been included in the price of his ticket. Too late the man realized that he had been living far beneath his privileges.[41]

Imagine how sad it would be to discover that physical, emotional, and spiritual help was available from the Lord and that you qualified for that help—yet you chose not to take advantage of it.

Elizabeth Endured Trials of Rejection

After twenty years of marriage, Elizabeth's husband announced that he wanted a divorce. Elizabeth knew that there were problems in the relationship, but she had no idea they were bad enough to warrant a divorce. Her husband, Ed, had a girlfriend on the side, and he wanted a divorce so

---
[41] Dieter F. Uchtdorf, "Your Potential, Your Privilege," *Ensign*, May 2011.

that he could be with his paramour. Elizabeth had a nervous breakdown from which she recovered.

Ed was able to hire an attorney to convince the judge to give him primary custody of their five children because Elizabeth had no financial reserves and no particular employable skills. She was a wife, a mother, and a homemaker. When Ed began depriving her of her visitation rights with the children, Elizabeth panicked and began calling Ed, yelling at him over the phone. Ed recorded the messages—and once again Ed's lawyer was able to convince the judge that Elizabeth was emotionally unstable and therefore should have only supervised visitation rights with her children.

Ed had the money and the power, and he eventually took the children to another state and cut off all contact between Elizabeth and her children. He monitored the mail and destroyed all the letters that Elizabeth sent to her children.

It was at that point that John met Elizabeth. She had every reason to be depressed and discouraged. The legal system had failed her, and now she had no contact with her children. She had been given the house in the divorce, but she could not afford to make the monthly payments on it and was forced to sell it. She was living off the money from the sale of the house and renting an apartment. She estimated she would run out of money in three years. Elizabeth had been a faithful member of the Church but didn't feel that she fit in anymore.

Elizabeth was quite attractive, and her married friends abandoned her when she divorced. Some saw her as a single female who was a potential threat to their own marriages. Elizabeth was confident that God had abandoned her, and in her desperation, she had contemplated suicide.

John's counsel to Elizabeth was to take control over the things she could control rather than focusing on all of the things that were out of her control. John explained to her the concept of wishes versus goals. John suggested that we define a goal as something over which we have control. Weight loss is a good example. A wish is something that depends on other people. Her husband giving her permission to visit the children would be an example of a wish. We began to focus on Elizabeth's goals to put her own spiritual house in order, get a job, and become independent.

John promised her that the Lord could and would divinely intervene if she were willing to be humble and diligent and exercise the prayer of faith. That wasn't John's promise—it was the Lord's promise. Resenting the Lord only made things worse for Elizabeth. The Lord is her ally and is more powerful than Ed and an army of lawyers. Elizabeth agreed to get on the pathway to obtaining a temple recommend. She started to pray again, she became active in Relief Society, and she started her own house-cleaning business. Soon she hired three different women to help in the business. All this happened in the course of one year.

As Elizabeth became spiritually and financially stable, I asked her to keep a special notebook containing photocopies of every letter she sent her children. Her oldest child, a daughter, would soon turn sixteen, and under the laws of the state of Utah, the child could choose the parent with whom she wanted to live. If the court determines that the parent is stable, the court grants permission for a change of custody. Elizabeth prayed every night and was diligent and humble before the Lord. Feeling hope for the first time, she felt physically, emotionally, and spiritually strengthened.

Elizabeth met her sixteen-year-old daughter, Carrie, at her ex-mother-in-law's home in Salt Lake. The first question Carrie asked was, "Why didn't you contact us?" Elizabeth produced photocopies of the letters she had sent each week to each of her children for the past year. Carrie was stunned. Her father had told her that Elizabeth was insane and had been hospitalized in American Fork. When Carrie realized that her father had been lying to her, she broke down and cried because she loved her mother. The courts determined that Elizabeth was stable; she had a small, successful business and was able to provide for her children.

Carrie was the first of the children to return to live with her mother. This saga played out over a period of ten years when the last of the children, a set of twins, turned sixteen. All five children returned to live with their mother.

Elizabeth told John that she was physically, emotionally, and spiritually strengthened and found comfort in taking her frustrations to the Lord. She stopped complaining to anyone who would listen to her. Elizabeth stopped trying to be the victim. She did what she could in terms of writing letters and making photocopies of them. She felt comfortable trusting in the Lord, which required patience and faith as well as humility, diligence, and prayer.

Alma Faced Overwhelming Odds

Alma and the people of Zarahemla faced overwhelming odds. A large group of Nephite dissenters had joined with the Lamanites. The Book of Mormon describes them as

> being as numerous almost, as it were, as the sands of the sea. . . .

> Nevertheless, the Nephites being strengthened by the hand of the Lord, having prayed mightily to him that he would deliver them out of the hands of their enemies, therefore the Lord did hear their cries, and did strengthen them, and the Lamanites and the Amlicites did fall before them. (Alma 2:27–28)

During this same battle, Alma fought Amlici face to face.

> And it came to pass that Alma, being a man of God, being exercised with much faith, cried, saying: O Lord, have mercy and spare my life, that I may be an instrument in thy hands to save and preserve this people.
>
> Now when Alma had said these words he contended again with Amlici; and he was strengthened, insomuch that he slew Amlici with the sword. (Alma 2:30–31)

The relationship between prayer and being strengthened is blatantly obvious. On another occasion, 450 converts, comprised of families, had listened to and accepted Alma's teachings about Christ. Wicked King Noah considered Alma a troublemaker and sent an army to destroy him and his followers. Alma was made aware of the king's army and fled into the wilderness (see Mosiah 18:33–34), where he and his people "gathered together their flocks, and took of their grain, and departed in the wilderness before the armies of king Noah" (Mosiah 23:1). They should have been an easy group to overtake. It seems absurd to think that old and young, women and small children, weighed down by flocks and grain could out-march an entire army. But look at what happened next: "And the Lord did strengthen them, that the people of king Noah could not overtake them to destroy them. And they fled eight days' journey into the wilderness" (Mosiah 23:2–3). As mentioned, in addition to providing physical strength, the Lord will emotionally and spiritually strengthen those who call on Him in mighty prayer. After seeing the apostasy of the Zoramites, Alma pleaded with the Lord for emotional and spiritual strength:

> O Lord God, how long wilt thou suffer that such wickedness and infidelity shall be among this people? O Lord, wilt thou give me strength, that I may bear with mine infirmities. For I am infirm, and such wickedness among this people doth pain my soul.

> O Lord, my heart is exceedingly sorrowful; wilt thou comfort my soul in Christ. O Lord, wilt thou grant unto me that I may have strength, that I may suffer with patience these afflictions which shall come upon me, because of the iniquity of this people.
>
> O Lord, wilt thou comfort my soul, and give unto me success, and also my fellow laborers who are with me . . . even all these wilt thou comfort, O Lord. Yea, wilt thou comfort their souls in Christ.
>
> Wilt thou grant unto them that they may have strength, that they may bear their afflictions which shall come upon them because of the iniquities of this people.
>
> . . . Now this was according to the prayer of Alma; and this because he prayed in faith. (Alma 31:30–33, 38).

Alma pleaded with the Lord for spiritual and emotional support for his soul, which was pained because of the poor choices of his once-beloved Nephite brethren. The Lord has not changed. The same spiritual and emotional support that was given to Alma is available to us today. The formula is still the same. As we take our love to our loved ones and approach the Lord with humility, diligence, and the prayer of faith, God will strengthen us emotionally and spiritually so that we can endure the poor choices of those we love. We also have to learn to curb our tongues and not speak poorly to anyone about our loved ones except to the Lord in prayer.

The more you focus on trying to change a loved one, the more frustrated you will become. The more you focus on emphasizing the positive about your loved one, thereby showing acceptance and appreciation, the more successful you will be. By turning the responsibility of changing the heart of your loved one over to the Lord, you are free to focus on what you can do to improve the relationship.

Stand Your Ground

If you have ever played volleyball, you know how frustrating it can be when people leave their assigned areas. This often happens when some of the better players lack confidence in their teammates and try to play two positions. Quite often the ball will land in the area that was abandoned by the better player.

That applies to life as well as volleyball. We need to stand our ground and stay within our assigned areas. The Lord has assigned us the responsibility to love and be a source of acceptance, affection, and appreciation for our loved ones. When we abandon that assignment and decide to take over the Lord's role of changing the heart by using uninspired criticism or inspired criticism inappropriately given, we are demonstrating a lack of faith in Christ. When we leave our assigned areas, we may gain a point or two, but it is more likely that we will lose the game. We may also lose a point or two because of less gifted players, but in the end, because the Lord is on our side, we will be victorious. Stand your ground.

Christina was a devoted mother who married young and out of the Church. Her husband, Fred, was a good provider and a caring father but was not interested in the Church. They had two boys followed by a girl. As her children began to grow up, Christina wanted to take them to Primary and expose them to the teachings of the Church. Fred didn't mind as long as Christina took responsibility for getting the children to and from the meetinghouse.

Sunday was a play day for Fred and a time for him to enjoy all different kinds of sports. Soon, the two boys decided it was more fun to be with dad on Sunday. Fred and Christina's daughter, Patsy, continued to go to church with her mother.

Fred smoked outside the house, but there were always a couple of beers in the refrigerator. Though the boys were baptized, they grew up in Fred's world. When her boys started smoking and drinking as teenagers, Christina blamed Fred, and it became a source of constant friction and contention.

Christina also blamed herself and felt like a failure. In Christina's mind, the teachings of the Church to become an eternal family became a myth. It wasn't long before the stress and contention took a toll on Christina's physical health. Her relationship with Fred and her two sons was a daily and all-consuming concern.

It was at this point that John was approached to see if he could help with the marriage. Fred wanted to blame the Church. Christina wanted to blame Fred. John asked to meet with them individually. Fred was upset that his wife had become such a nag; he was considering divorce so he could have some peace in his life. Christina was living with constant frustration, feelings of failure, and physical illness.

Over time, John was able to share with Christina some practical skills. He explained to Christina that all frustration comes from unmet expectations. There is no such thing as frustration in someone who doesn't have an expectation. He asked Christina to make a wish list of all the things she wanted to change in the lives of her loved ones. Her list was predictable. She wanted Fred to join the Church, and she wanted to be sealed to him and her children in the temple. She wanted her two boys and Patsy to also partake of temple blessings.

When John told her to let go of trying to personally see that these things would happen, she burst into tears. She thought he wanted her to let go of her dreams, wishes, and ideals. He didn't. What John wanted her to let go of was the method she was using to attain her ideal outcome. He wanted her to stand her ground. What she was doing wasn't fulfilling her heart-felt wishes. Nagging about Fred's smoking and drinking, blaming Fred for the two boys doing the same, and in general not being a pleasant person whom others wanted to be around was counterproductive and ineffective.

When John explained the concept of taking her love to her loved ones and taking all her frustrations to the Lord, Christina seemed puzzled at first. John could tell that Christina loved the Lord and had sufficient faith to trust Jesus. John went through a series of "what-ifs" with Christina. What if you turned the responsibility for changing your loved ones completely over to the Lord? What if you didn't nag Fred anymore about his smoking and drinking? What if you didn't nag the boys, either? What if you knew that the Lord would bring about these changes in His own time?

John asked her to imagine that she was meeting with the Savior. He asked her to imagine that the Lord told her everything would work out for the eternal best interest of Fred and their two sons. Next, John asked her to imagine that the Lord gave her an assignment: she was to stop all negative communications—no more nagging, no more contention, no more criticism. John asked Christina to imagine that the Lord laid His hands on her head and gave her a blessing that He would change their hearts *if* she were willing to take her love to her family members and all her frustrations to the Lord in prayer. She was to be patient and long-suffering and trust in the Lord. Then John asked Christina, "Would you do it?" John asked her to pray about it to see if that is what the Lord wanted her to do.

Christina returned later and said she would try, but she feared she would not be able to do it. John asked her if she really wanted the alternative—for things to stay as they were or to get worse, a scenario that included divorce. Sometimes divorce is the answer when there is physical abuse or emotional abuse. Constant criticism is a form of verbal abuse. Christina's nagging was verbal abuse, and it wasn't working. The Lord will not ask you to stay in a relationship where your soul can be destroyed. Nor would the Lord ever ask you to do that which is illegal or immoral. In this case, Christina needed to let go of being the change agent by standing her ground and being a loving person. She needed to let the Lord be the change agent.

John explained to Christina that once you change one side of a math formula, the other side has to change. The same is true in human relationships.

"Christina, you are one-half of every relationship to which you are a party," he told her. "If you will change your half of the relationship, the other half will have to change as well. How badly do you want the Lord to take care of Fred and your two sons? This is all about trusting the Lord. The key is for you to be humble and prayerful and trust in the Lord. You need to be diligent in being a positive person—not perfect, but quickly returning to the positive as soon as possible. Fred loves you, but right now he and the boys want peace in their lives. If you are unwilling to do this, you will be divorced and the two boys will live with Fred, leaving you and your daughter, Patsy, alone."

When meeting with Fred alone, John asked him if he would be willing to let Christina invite him to join her in Church-related activities. John explained that Christina would be free to invite him and that he would be free to say no to every invitation.

"Won't she be mad if I say no all the time?" he asked.

"No; she has already agreed that she wants to feel free to invite you and you can feel free to say no," John told him.

He agreed somewhat skeptically to try. John assured him that Christina was going to stop nagging about his smoking and drinking and that she would also stop nagging the boys. Fred expressed the thought that his teenage sons should not be smoking and drinking and voiced concern about his poor example. John explained that it would be up to him to work on that issue with the boys. Christina was not going to mention it anymore. Again, Fred was skeptical.

Once John had a firm commitment from Christina to find ways of showing acceptance, affection, and appreciation to her husband and sons, John met with Fred and Christina together. They went over some ground rules for their relationship. They included "Seven Articles of Commitment to Myself and My Mate" in the form of a contract that they each agreed to sign.

Seven Articles of Commitment to Me and My Mate

Article 1: I am willing to admit there are areas of strength as well as areas of weakness in our relationship, and I am willing to work on both maximizing our strengths and minimizing our weaknesses.

Article 2: I am willing to assume responsibility for my behavior, to own it. I choose to act and to react. I have 100 percent responsibility over my half of any relationship to which I am a party.

Article 3: I am willing to commit to a sincere effort to improve my communication skills and to be a greater source of affection, acceptance, and appreciation.

Article 4: I am willing to forgive my mate for all past wrongs, hurt feelings, and personal heartaches as of this date.

Article 5: I am willing to rededicate myself to a renewed effort to be a better me, in spite of any feelings of personal inadequacy or past failures.

Article 6: I am willing to refrain from speaking ill of my mate to friend, family, or stranger. I will not embarrass or belittle my mate in front of others nor will I be critical of my mate in his or her absence. I will also ask for my mate's permission to criticize him or her.

Article 7: I am willing to agree that I will commit myself to a ninety-day wholehearted effort to honor these commitments. If I fail, I will start my ninety days over again. At the end of ninety successful days, I will honestly evaluate my progress.

Signature	Date	Signature	Date

Willingness leads to solutions; unwillingness defeats all solutions. Fred and Christina's relationship began to improve immediately. Christina had hope in Christ, and Fred had peace at home. As time went by, Fred's skepticism vanished. He was genuinely appreciative of Christina's changed attitude. Christina and Patsy met every night to pray together. One night, Fred asked if he could join them. Christina was wise enough not to ask Fred to pray but was content just to have him there.

On Sundays, Christina asked Fred in a cheerful tone of voice, "Do you want to go to church today, big fella?"

"No, but thanks for asking," Fred always responded.

One Sunday, Christina forgot to ask Fred if he wanted to go to church. Fred inquired, "Aren't you going to ask me to go to church?"

Christina asked, "Would you like to go to church?"

"No, but I don't want you to give up on me."

Over the next few years, Fred started playing basketball with the team at church. Eventually Fred gave up smoking and drinking and joined the Church. The boys didn't go on missions for the Church, and they eventually married less-active Latter-day Saint girls. The oldest boy was gradually influenced by his wife to become active in the Church. As of this date, the younger son remains firmly entrenched in the things of the world.

A few years ago, we were invited to attend a temple sealing. Fred, Christina, Patsy, and their oldest son were sealed in the Jordan River Temple. Fred stood as a witness as his eldest son was sealed to his wife and their two young children.

Now the entire efforts of Fred, Christina, Patsy, and the eldest son and his wife are focused on loving the second son. They do not criticize him or his wife. They have an understanding that they are free to invite the younger son to all of the family activities, such as the baptism of a nephew or niece, and he is free to say no—and no one will be offended on either side. The second son and his wife do participate in some family activities, especially during the holidays. Only the Lord knows what will happen next.

Let's go back and revisit Christina, who at one time was a nagging, critical, frustrated, and unhappy woman. Where would she be at this time had she persisted in her negative approach? And remember what was on her wish list? She wanted to be sealed to Fred in the temple and to have her children sealed to them. She may have to wait for the second son, but she does not have to wait to take her acceptance, affection, and appreciation to him.

The Prophet Joseph Smith said he was able to govern because, "I teach them correct principles and they govern themselves."[42] Taking your love and acceptance to a loved one and taking your frustrations to the Lord is a correct principle. It requires humility to trust that the Lord can do things you cannot do. It requires diligence, which often includes patience and long-suffering. It requires that you take your frustrations and concerns to the Lord in mighty prayer. Lastly, it requires that you cease finding fault with your loved ones and focus on the positive in their lives.

John asked Christina what it felt like to let go and to let God handle it. She said it was scary. She stated that once she truly committed to letting the Lord change the hearts of her loved ones, she felt relieved. She was also spiritually comforted and emotionally strengthened.

There are multiple examples in the scriptures of how the Lord strengthens His children. Let's look at just a few:

---

[42] James R. Clark, comp., *Messages of the First Presidency* (Salt Lake City: Bookcraft, 1965–1975), 3:54.

And thus we see that the commandments of God must be fulfilled. And if it so be that the children of men keep the commandments of God he doth nourish them, and strengthen them, and provide means whereby they can accomplish the thing which he has commanded them. (1 Nephi 17:3)

Yea, in the strength of the Lord we did go forth to battle against the Lamanites; for I and my people did cry mightily to the Lord that he would deliver us. . . .
And God did hear our cries and did answer our prayers. (Mosiah 9:17–18; see also Mosiah 10:10–11; Alma 2:18, 28)

And I will also ease the burdens which are put upon your shoulders, that even you cannot feel them upon your backs. . . .
And now it came to pass that the burdens which were laid upon Alma and his brethren were made light; yea, the Lord did strengthen them that they could bear up their burdens with ease, and they did submit cheerfully and with patience to all the will of the Lord. (Mosiah 24:14–15)

O Lord, give us strength according to our faith which is in Christ, even unto deliverance. And they broke the cords with which they were bound. . . . (Alma 14:26)

[Lachoneus, the governor,] did cause that his people should cry unto the Lord for strength against the time that the robbers should come down against them. (3 Nephi 3:12)

Just as He did for the people in the scriptures, the Lord is willing to strengthen you or your loved one physically, spiritually and emotionally when invited by prayer to do so.

The Third Principle of Divine Intervention: Raising Someone Up to Do What We Cannot Do

On occasion, the Lord may make a direct appearance to a Moses or a Paul. More often He sends angels, prophets, and Church leaders. By far the most common "someone" who is raised up by the Lord is an imperfect person.

We are all examples of imperfect people who are trying to help other imperfect people. Often the person who is raised up by the Lord to be an instrument in His hands to bless the life of another is unaware that he or she is that instrument. For example, in the Book of Mormon there was a man named Gideon who had a plan to deliver the people of Limhi from bondage (see Mosiah 22:3–8).

Gideon had a plan, but was unaware that his plan was inspired by the Lord: "Now the name of the man was Gideon; and it was he who was an instrument in the hands of God in delivering the people of Limhi out of bondage" (Alma 1:8). Let's look at some of the more popular and obvious examples in the scriptures of the Lord raising people up.

Moses and Aaron Raised Up to Deliver the Hebrew Nation

When Moses was on Mount Sinai, the Lord told him to go to Pharaoh with the request to "Let my people go" (Exodus 8:1).

Moses responded, "Who am I, that I should go unto Pharaoh, and that I should bring forth the children of Israel out of Egypt?" (Exodus 3:11). Moses attempted to convince the Lord that he was the wrong person to send. Moses pleaded, "they will not believe me, nor hearken unto my voice . . ." (Exodus 4:1). The Lord assured Moses that He would provide signs to Pharaoh that would convince Pharaoh. Moses's final appeal was to tell the Lord, "I am not eloquent, neither heretofore, nor since thou hast spoken unto thy servant: but I am slow of speech, and of a slow tongue" (Exodus 4:10).

None of Moses's objections impressed the Lord. The Lord raised up Aaron, the brother of Moses, to be the spokesperson for Moses. So Moses was raised up to help the Hebrew nation, and Aaron was raised up to help Moses (see Exodus 4:10–16).

What has been said about Moses being raised up to be an instrument in the hands of the Lord can be said of each of the dispensational heads, including Adam and Eve, Abel, Enoch (see Moses 7:1–2), Noah (see Genesis 7:1), Abraham (see Genesis 12:1–2), Peter (see Matthew 16:18), and Joseph Smith (see D&C 1:17).

Our Heavenly Father sent prophets in all of these dispensations with the voice of warning for the wicked and a voice of comfort to strengthen the righteous. In both Peter's dispensation and our current dispensation, the Lord has sent Apostles and prophets to direct the affairs of His Church (see Ephesians 4:11–13).

Have Angels Ceased to Appear?

The principles of divine intervention as they relate to the Lord raising someone up involve entire nations as well as the individual child of God. The Lord uses angels to carry His messages to individuals. After Adam was driven out of the Garden of Eden, he was commanded to offer the firstlings of the flocks for an offering to the Lord. After many days, an angel of the Lord appeared to Adam and explained to him that the sacrifice was a similitude of the Only Begotten of the Father (see Moses 5:7). Angels appeared to Hagar (see Genesis 16:7–13) and Abraham (see Genesis 22:11) and prepared the way for Abraham's servant to select the wife for Isaac (see Genesis 24:7, 40). Three angels came to Lot in Sodom (see Joseph Smith Translation, Exodus 19:1, footnote a). Jacob saw angels ascending and descending a ladder in the heaven (see Genesis 28:12). Gideon, Job, and Elijah all entertained angels. There are more than fifty additional references in the Old Testament alone to angels.

In the New Testament, the angel Gabriel appeared to both Zacharias in Jerusalem (see Luke 1:11) and Mary at Nazareth (see Luke 1:26–27). Jesus had angels minister to Him after the temptations and in the Garden of Gethsemane. There are dozens of additional references to angels in the New Testament.

Equally, the Book of Mormon is replete with examples of angels. These angels appeared to righteous Nephi as well as to his unrighteous brothers (see 1 Nephi 3:29–30). Among the dozens of angelic visitations in the Book of Mormon, one of our favorites is the angel that appeared to unrighteous Alma the Younger (see Mosiah 27:11–17). Alma and the four sons of Mosiah were described as "the very vilest of sinners" (Mosiah 28:4). Alma the younger "became a very wicked and an idolatrous man. . . . he was going about to destroy the church of God, for he did go about secretly with the sons of Mosiah . . . rebelling against God" (Mosiah 27:8, 10–11).

The angel told Alma that he had come in response to the prayers of Alma's father. It brings great comfort to our souls to think that we could pray and the Lord would raise up angels to divinely intervene in the lives of our children and grandchildren. Mormon asked the following question:

> Have angels ceased to appear unto the children of men? . . . Or will [they], so long as time shall last, or the earth shall stand, or there shall be one man upon the face thereof to be saved?
>
> Behold I say unto you, Nay; for it is by faith that miracles are wrought; and it is by faith that angels appear and minister

unto men; wherefore, if these things have ceased wo be unto
the children of men, for it is because of unbelief, and all is
vain. (Moroni 7:36–37)

We are confident in the knowledge that the Lord will send an angel when necessary. In his letter to the Hebrews, Paul encouraged brotherly love toward strangers, saying that "some have entertained angels unawares" (Hebrews 13:2). We are told that the three translated Nephites will be among the Gentiles, the Jews, those of scattered Israel, and among all nations, kindreds, tongues, and people, who will "know them not" (3 Nephi 28:27). It also mentions that the Three Nephites "can show themselves unto whatsoever man it seemeth them good" (3 Nephi 28:30).

In John's patriarchal blessing, he was told that the Lord had His angels watching over him since his birth. To John's knowledge, he has never entertained an angel. However, there have been angels in his life. John was the only person in his immediate family who was a member of the Church, but John had a stake president, Herbert Anderson, who watched over him from the time he was twelve until he went on a mission at age nineteen. Another angel was Leslie Gilbert. Back then, we had "ward teachers," very much the same as ministering brothers today. From the time John was twelve until he was sixteen, Brother Gilbert would not let him escape the responsibility of visiting the families they had been assigned to visit each month—a responsibility with a territory that covered ninety miles. Brother Gilbert later became John's bishop and made it a point to make friends with John's parents, neither of whom were members of the Church.

Does the Lord send angels in our day and time? Yes, we believe He does. But why send an angel if a ministering sister, a ministering brother, a Primary teacher, or a bishop will do? Sometimes our friends and other family members are the ones raised up to be instruments in the hands of the Lord. Lehi counseled Laman and Lemuel:

> Rebel no more against your brother, whose views have been glorious, and who hath kept the commandments from the time that we left Jerusalem; and who hath been an instrument in the hands of God, in bringing us forth into the land of promise; for were it not for him, we must have perished with hunger in the wilderness. . . . (2 Nephi 1:24)

The once-wicked four sons of Mosiah (Ammon, Aaron, Omner, and Himni) repented and eventually converted thousands to the Lord. They went forth

> . . . zealously striving to repair all the injuries which they had done to the church, confessing all their sins, and publishing all the things which they had seen, and explaining the prophecies and the scriptures to all who desired to hear them.
>
> And thus they were instruments in the hands of God in bringing many to the knowledge of the truth, yea, to the knowledge of their Redeemer. (Mosiah 27:35–36)

> And the Lord said unto them also: Go forth among the Lamanites, thy brethren, and establish my word; yet ye shall be patient in long-suffering and afflictions, that ye may show forth good examples unto them in me, and I will make an instrument of thee in my hands unto the salvation of many souls. (Alma 17:11)

Being an instrument in the hands of the Lord almost always requires being "patient and long-suffering." The suffering we may have to endure is watching our loved ones make poor choices with all their subsequent consequences. As painful as it may be to watch them, it may be necessary for them to learn by the things that they suffer (see D&C 105:6). In truth, we do not need to sit on our hands. We can actively take our love and acceptance to them and pray mightily to our Heavenly Father to intervene.

The great temptation is to rescue our loved ones from the consequences of their poor choices. In all our efforts, we need to be sure that our intervention is guided by the Holy Ghost. A lesson each of us must learn is to accept responsibility for the choices we make. Blaming someone else for choices we make may justify us in our own minds, but it does not convince our conscience or God. "Passing the buck" doesn't work. When Adam was asked why he partook of the forbidden fruit, he blamed Eve. When Eve was asked why she partook of the forbidden fruit, she said that the devil made her do it. When Satan was asked what happened, he tried to justify his behavior. The Lord held each accountable.

Nell the Shoplifting Teenager

Some things go hand in hand. Shoplifting and lying are two of them. *Shoplifting* is a euphemistic term for "stealing." When Nell was nine years old, she stole several candy bars from a corner grocery store. When her mother, Betty, found out about it, she scolded Nell, but there were no consequences. What Betty should have done was to take Nell back to the store, have her return the remaining candy, apologize, and agree to pay for it. Betty should have loaned the money to Nell but then required Nell to do several small jobs around the house to earn the money.

As a teenager, Nell started stealing clothes. She wanted to be popular and resented the fact that her parents didn't give her enough money to buy the best clothes. Nell felt justified. When she was arrested, her parents pleaded with the judge and promised to repay her debts and to supervise Nell more closely. It probably would have been better for Nell to have spent a night in jail and perform twenty hours of community service as a consequence for her shoplifting. At eighteen, Nell could have petitioned the courts to have her juvenile record expunged. Nell's parents were held hostage by their fears that Nell might not be able to qualify for a scholarship. The parents were embarrassed and wanted to suppress the reality that their daughter was a thief.

What did Nell learn from all of this? She learned that you could avoid the consequences if you pled with the judge. She learned that if you were emotional enough, if you cried a lot, or if you lied about it, you might be able to avoid the consequences.

After she turned eighteen, Nell was caught shoplifting. This time, all of her tears and her promises not to do it again were of no avail. Nell now has a police record; fortunately, it is for a misdemeanor. This means she can still vote as a citizen. If she were convicted of felony theft, she wouldn't be able to vote and would not be able to work at any facility that requires a criminal background check.

Nell is at a crossroads in her life. She can accept responsibility for her poor choices or she can continue to blame others, rationalize, and justify her inappropriate behavior. Her parents are also at a crossroads. Will they continue to be enablers? Will they continue to save Nell from herself? At some point, both Nell and her parents need to transfer responsibility for Nell's choices squarely to her. Nell and her parents are the only ones who can write the ending to this story.

It should be the goal of every parent to help their child become his or her highest and best self, and to do it in a manner consistent with the teachings of Jesus Christ. Sometimes, despite our best efforts, we remain unsurprisingly imperfect.

A Tale of Two Peoples

Fortunately, the Lord does not require us to be perfect in order to enjoy His divine intervention. The previously mentioned people of Limhi were slow to hearken to the Lord and call upon Him in prayer:

> And now the Lord was slow to hear their cry because of their iniquities; nevertheless the Lord did hear their cries, and began to soften the hearts of the Lamanites that they began to ease their burdens; yet the Lord did not see fit to deliver them out of bondage.
>
> And it came to pass that they began to prosper by degrees in the land.... (Mosiah 21:15–16)

Despite the imperfections and iniquities of the Lamanites, the Lord intervened to soften their hearts because of their eventual humility and prayer. Prior to their being sufficiently humble, the people of King Limhi had brought upon themselves this bondage because of their wickedness.

The people of Limhi were assisted by the Lord gradually as they turned away from their wickedness. The story of Alma and his people is different: they were a righteous people who were brought into bondage. Their story reminds us that both the wicked and the righteous face adversity in this life. The difference is the degree to which the Lord divinely intervenes to strengthen and deliver the righteous.

After the people of Alma had out-marched the armies of wicked King Noah, they established themselves and prospered in the land they called Helam. While there, they were discovered by a lost army of King Noah—not the same army that had previously pursued them—who had been looking for the people of Limhi. During the many days this lost army was wandering in the wilderness they discovered a community of wicked priests of King Noah who fled into the wilderness after the death of King Noah. These priests had kidnapped twenty-four of the daughters of the Lamanites and taken them as wives. The leader of these twenty-four families of priests was Amulon. He was well acquainted with Alma and hated him for believing the words of the prophet Abinadi.

Amulon joined with the lost army of King Noah in search of the land of Nephi. To their surprise, they discovered the people of Alma in the land of Helam. Alma knew the way back to the land of Nephi. He agreed to tell them how to get back to the land of Nephi if they would grant his people their lives and freedom. In spite of their promise, the lost army and the people of Amulon subjugated the people of Alma and treated them as slaves.

Limhi's People	Alma's People
The afflictions of the Nephites were great, and there was no way that they could deliver themselves, for the Lamanites had surrounded them on every side (see Mosiah 21:5).	King Laman exercised authority over them, put tasks upon them, and put taskmasters over them (see Mosiah 24:9).
The people began to murmur and complain. Three times they went to war and lost. They cried mightily from day to day, but not unto the Lord (see Mosiah 21:6–12).	The people of Alma did not murmur or complain. They cried mightily unto God, but were forbidden to pray vocally on threat of death (see Mosiah 24:10–11).
After the third defeat, they humbled themselves to the dust and began to call upon the Lord (see Mosiah 21:12–14).	Alma and his people prayed unto the Lord from their hearts even though they had been forbidden to pray vocally (see Mosiah 24:10–12).
The Lord was slow to hear their cries because of their iniquity, but began to soften the hearts of the Lamanites (see Mosiah 21:15).	The voice of the Lord came to them promising deliverance and strengthening them (see Mosiah 24:13–14).
Inspired by the Lord, Gideon got the guards drunk; with Ammon, he led the people to Zarahemla (see Mosiah 22:3–11).	The Lord caused a deep sleep to come upon the guards. Alma and his people escaped to Zarahemla (see Mosiah 24:19–25).
The people began to prosper by degrees (see Mosiah 21:16).	Great was their faith and patience (see Mosiah 24:16).

Rather than murmur and complain, as did the people of Limhi, the people of Alma remained humble and prayerful. The Lord heard their prayers, eased the burdens upon their backs, and delivered them by causing a deep sleep to come upon their captors so that the people of Alma could escape and return to the land of Zarahemla. Contrast the deliverance of the people of Alma with the deliverance of the people of Limhi (see Mosiah 21–24). For example, the Lord caused a deep sleep to come upon the guards so that Alma and his group could escape. Limhi's plan involved getting the guards drunk.

In His goodness, the Lord responds to all His children. We read that the Lord "cannot look upon sin with the least degree of allowance" (D&C 1:31). However, our Heavenly Father looks upon His children with a great degree of allowance conditioned upon their humility, their prayers of faith, and their willingness to improve.

Both the people of Limhi and the people of Alma were brought into bondage, with no way to deliver themselves. Limhi's people tried delivering themselves out of bondage. Three battles and considerable loss of life later, they were left with a multitude of widows. Earlier a group of people were chastised because they were compelled by circumstances to be humble instead of truly humbling themselves (see Alma 32:14) without being compelled by circumstances to do so.

Alma and his people were brought into bondage as a test of their faith. They were humble and prayerful before, during, and after they were in bondage. Limhi and his people became humble and prayerful only after having exhausted all their alternatives. It is important to note that the Lord did respond to both groups and did deliver both groups when they were humble and prayerful.

The Fourth Principle of Divine Intervention: The Exodus Principle

The word *exodus* means to depart, to lead away. When we hear *exodus*, most of us think of Moses leading the people of Israel out of Egypt and into the promised land. Technically, the Lord leading Adam and Eve out of the Garden of Eden was an exodus. The Jaredites were led away from the Tower of Babel. Abraham was led away from his apostate father's home in Haran to the land of Canaan (modern-day Israel and Palestine). Lehi was led away from Jerusalem before the Babylonians took it captive. Sometimes the Lord will lead a person out of a bad marriage. That is also an exodus principle.

The key, of course, is that the exodus is inspired by the Lord and not by frustration alone.

The Lord looks after the interest of all of His children. So before there is an Exodus, there is an attempt or several attempts by the Lord to soften the heart of both parties. In the case of Moses and Pharaoh, there were ten attempts—called the ten plagues—to soften Pharaoh's heart. The Lord's patience and long-suffering with even the most wicked of His children may require that we also must be patient and longsuffering before the Lord will lead us out of a difficult situation. Cain, who eventually became a son of perdition, was approached by the Lord before he ever became a son of perdition. The Lord told Cain, "If thou doest well, thou shalt be accepted. And if thou doest not well, sin lieth at the door, and Satan desireth to have thee" (Moses 5:23).

It is a highly unlikely and an extremely remote possibility that any of us will have a son, daughter, or other family member qualify to become a son of perdition. Murder does not make one a son of perdition. Actively seeking to destroy the Atonement with an absolute sure knowledge of its truthfulness coupled with loving Lucifer more than our Heavenly Father qualifies one to be a son of perdition. As lost and as fallen as our loved one may be, he or she is not beyond the grace and mercy of God.

To Leave or Not to Leave: Beverly and Phil

Phil was a skilled and successful dentist with a lucrative practice in southern California. Phil lived in a bit of a bubble. Everyone in his office knew their own success depended on *his* success, so he was used to being obeyed without question. Imagine working in an environment where everyone around you responded to all of your directives.

Unfortunately, Dr. Phil expected that same kind of response from his wife, Beverly. When he didn't get it, he became critical and found fault. After all, he had provided her a lovely home in the nicest part of town. She had her own BMW, a closet full of beautiful clothes, and a maid who came in one day a week.

Phil hurled a veritable shopping list of criticisms at Beverly on a daily basis. He was critical of her weight, even though she was only about ten pounds overweight. Beverly had a big house and a housekeeper who came in once a week to do the deep cleaning. Phil expected the house to be in such a condition that *Better Homes and Gardens* could show up unannounced and photograph it at any time. While Beverly did her best, there was always a little clutter left somewhere by their four children.

Phil ranted about Beverly letting the kids eat popcorn or anything else in her car; eating was supposed to happen in the kitchen. That brought up another criticism from Phil: Beverly was a terrible cook, and he expected her to sit down and plan the meals a week in advance and go to the store to purchase that food. Beverly tried, but she gave up because the kids were always eating the ingredients she needed to prepare any given meal. Phil wanted to eat exactly at six every evening, and the children's schedules often made that impossible. Phil often found a note on the refrigerator saying to heat his dinner in the microwave.

As far as Church service was concerned, Phil was on the high council and Beverly was a counselor in the Young Women's presidency.

It was a constant source of frustration to Phil that when he called home, Beverly was usually talking to her friends on the phone. He resented the fact that Beverly had so many friends. Phil accused her of being a poor mother. He felt that she should spend less time on the phone and more quality time with the children.

Beverly had an interest in art and attended an art class once a week at the local community college. Phil reluctantly took over the responsibility of watching the children while Beverly was at her art class. The children hated it when Beverly went to the art class because Phil wouldn't let them watch television until they had cleaned up their rooms, helped straighten up the house, washed any dishes they may have taken to their rooms, focused on practicing their musical instruments, and finished their homework. He also confiscated their phones until they finished all the work. Sure enough, when Beverly came home the house was ready to be photographed by *Better Homes and Gardens*.

Phil really didn't like the fact that Beverly was her own person. He wanted Beverly to be like him. She had drawn a line in the sand and told Phil that she was doing the best she could and he was going to have to live with his frustrations because she wasn't willing to do any more than she was doing. Through it all, it was a complete mystery to Phil why Beverly was reluctant to have more physical intimacy with him.

Beverly had contacted a lawyer and was ready to exit the relationship. Beverly wondered if she had ever loved Phil or if Phil had ever really loved her. Criticism had erased the love that brought them to be sealed in the Los Angeles Temple so many years earlier.

This was the circumstance under which John was called in to help. He had solutions for all of Phil and Beverly's issues; the only question was whether they had the willingness to follow counsel.

This story has two potential outcomes. The first option is for Phil to reevaluate his priorities and become a source of acceptance, affection, and appreciation for Beverly. If he was unwilling to do that and persisted in his criticism, the second option was for the Lord to lead Beverly out of this verbally and emotionally unhealthy and abusive marriage.

It is difficult to summarize several counseling sessions wherein solutions were presented to Phil and Beverly. Here were the practical solutions to which Beverly agreed: Phil was not to verbally criticize Beverly anymore—not one word. If he had a criticism, he was to treat her as an equal and ask her for permission to share that criticism. He had to write the criticism down on paper or in a text message, but not without first obtaining her permission to receive it. He had to completely let go of certain issues that were taboo—Beverly's weight, her mothering skills, her art class, and her talking on the phone or texting her friends. Phil also needed to agree that the BMW was Beverly's car and she could do with it as she pleased.

As far as the house was concerned Phil, could choose any three rooms other than the kitchen that he wanted kept clean. Phil chose the living room, his office, and their bedroom. Beverly agreed, which meant she had to move some of her art supplies to an extra bedroom and turn it into a craft room. If Phil wanted to personally spend time cleaning, he was welcome to do so as long as he maintained a good attitude.

Beverly agreed to have three planned dinners a week. They agreed on Sunday, Tuesday, and Thursday. She would maintain sufficient food on hand, but the family would have to fend for themselves if they didn't like what she fixed on the other days. They would deal with physical intimacy as a separate matter.

As a part of the spiritual mending, Phil and Beverly agreed to pray together morning and night and re-commit to having a positive family home evening experience. That meant a ten- or fifteen-minute spiritual thought with the rest of the time spent playing video games or board games as a family.

John asked if both Phil and Beverly would be willing to follow through with these agreed-upon guidelines. An unwillingness on either part would spell failure. John was able to share a different perspective with Phil about righteous dominion. Together they read in Doctrine and Covenants 121:34–46 and in Moroni 7, and they discussed how to apply those principles, which involve persuasion, invitation, and enticement. It was time to change the pattern of threats and coercion. They also read *The Family: A Proclamation to the World*, in which fathers are counseled to preside over their families in love and righteousness. The Proclamation also advises that mothers and fathers are obligated to help one another as equal partners.

To help Phil remember that his wife and children were not employees he could simply order around, John asked him to wear a rubber band on his wrist when he went home at night. He was to snap it on his wrist as he put his hand on the doorknob to remind him that his wife was an "equal partner." Regarding the children, John encouraged him to invite, entice, and reward positive behavior. John assured Phil that the Lord would soften Beverly's heart as well as those of the children if he would take his love to his loved ones and at the same time take his frustrations to the Lord in personal and private prayer.

John had given Phil and Beverly the benefit of his education and training in resolving differences in healthy ways. It was now up to them.

Another possible ending to this story was an exodus experience for Beverly. If Phil remained or reverted to his critical nature after Beverly sincerely tried to fulfill her agreed-upon changes, the Lord would lead her out of that situation. After talking about that possibility, John's counsel to Beverly was to make sure that it was the Holy Ghost that led her away, not her eagerness to escape.

We wish every story had a fairytale ending. This one did not. Phil was fine for a while but gradually reverted to his critical nature. In Phil's mind, he was justified. He failed to grasp that *being* right was only half of what was needed. The other half was *acting* right. Phil is now a lone man in his own Garden of Eden.

The principle of exodus is alive and well today, as are all the principles of divine intervention—including the last one, which is to remove the problem.

The Fifth Principle of Divine Intervention: Removing the Problem

Historically, *removing the problem* seems to be the last resort for the Lord. Removing a person doesn't mean he or she will die, although in some cases the Lord does remove a person or an army to the spirit world. The key to any divine intervention is humility, diligence, and prayer.

Humility is not how you appear before your fellow man; it is how you appear before God. *Humility* is sometimes defined as a "broken heart and contrite spirit."[43] A broken heart is the opposite of a stubborn heart; a contrite

---

43 "Humble, Humility," Index to the Triple Combination.

spirit is one that is remorseful for being selfish. Humility is accepting God's will over our will and God's timing over our timing. The ultimate example is Christ, who in the Garden of Gethsemane uttered these words, "Father, If thou be willing, remove this cup from me: nevertheless not my will, but thine, be done" (Luke 22:42).

Allowing the Lord to divinely intervene and remove a problem means we need to be patient in our humility and diligently persist in calling upon the Lord in prayer. The scriptures provide the ultimate example: before the Lord removes a problem, considerable efforts are made to work with "the problem." Let's look at a few of those examples.

Sarah's Problem

The problem for Sarah was Hagar and Ishmael. We know that Sarah struggled for thirteen years before the problem was removed, though the scriptures do not tell us the degree of suffering that Sarah may have had to endure.

Sarah, the wife of Abraham, had a dilemma. She was barren and around seventy-six years old, well past childbearing years. In order for her husband to have seed, she gave him her handmaiden, Hagar, as his wife. By any standard, it took a great deal of love for Sarah to allow her husband to have another living wife.

After Hagar became pregnant with Ishmael, Hagar began to despise Sarah (see Genesis 16:5). Hagar should have been grateful and gracious, but she was not. Sarah confronted Abraham and said to him, "I have given my maid into thy bosom; and when she saw that she had conceived, I was despised in her eyes: the Lord judge between me and thee" (see Genesis 16:5). Abraham told Sarah to take care of the matter herself. Taking matters into her own hands, Sarah punished Hagar—at which point Hagar ran away. Influenced by the Lord, who told her she would bear a son named Ishmael, Hagar returned and spent the next thirteen years with Abraham, Sarah, and Ishmael.

Sarah miraculously conceived and gave birth to Isaac, but Ishmael became a threat to Sarah by mocking Isaac. Once again Sarah confronted Abraham and said, "Cast out this bondwoman and her son: for the son of this bondwoman shall not be heir with my son, even with Isaac. And the thing was very grievous in Abraham's sight because of his son [Ishmael]." (Genesis 21:10–11).

Things may have been grievous for Abraham, but the Lord supported Sarah and assured Abraham that things would go well for Hagar and Ishmael.

Abraham sent them away with bread and water, and Ishmael became an archer. After going through some trials, Hagar, an Egyptian, found an Egyptian woman to marry Ishmael. Eventually, Ishmael became the father of twelve princes and a multitude of people (see Genesis 16, 17, 21). The Arabs trace their lineage to Ishmael.

In this example, the Lord did remove Hagar and Ishmael, but did not destroy them.

Moses's Problem

The problem for Moses was Pharaoh. After ten plagues, the Lord gave Moses permission to take the children of Israel into the wilderness. As they were fleeing, they reached the shores of the Red Sea and saw that the chariots and army of Pharaoh were rapidly approaching and likely to overtake and destroy them. In one of the most amazing incidents in all of scripture, Moses parted the waters of the Red Sea by the power of God, and the Hebrew people crossed on dry land. As Pharaoh and his armies attempted to cross,

> . . . the waters returned, and covered the chariots, and the horsemen, and all the host of Pharaoh that came into the sea after them; there remained not so much as one of them.
>
> But the children of Israel walked upon dry land in the midst of the sea; and the waters were a wall unto them on their right hand, and on their left.
>
> Thus the Lord saved Israel that day out of the hand of the Egyptians; and Israel saw the Egyptians dead upon the sea shore. (Exodus 14:28–30)

Nephi's Problem

The problem for Nephi was Laban. The Lord had commanded Nephi to acquire the brass plates that contained the law of Moses and the writings of the holy prophets "since the world began" down to Jeremiah and the reign of Zedekiah. But just because the Lord wants something done doesn't mean that fulfilling the task will be quick and easy.

It seems quite unreasonable that a stranger would approach Laban and ask him to give up records in his possession unless that stranger was entitled to them. We do know that the genealogy of Lehi was on the plates of brass (see 1 Nephi 5:14, 16). Lacking the background information that may have been on the 116 lost pages of the Book of Mormon, we must resort to

Take Your Love to Your Family and Your Frustrations to the Lord

speculation. It is John's personal opinion that Lehi, if he were the oldest male in the extended family, was entitled to the records. Laban, who commanded a small army of fifty men, was the keeper of the family records.

In any case, Laman made the first attempt to obtain the plates of brass; when he did, Laban accused Laman of being a robber and threatened to kill him. Laman fled. Nephi then convinced Laman to collect their father's gold, silver, and precious things and offer them to Laban in exchange for the plates of brass. Seeing what the brothers were offering, Laban lusted after Lehi's property, thrust the brothers out again, and sent his servants to slay them (see 1 Nephi 3:22–25).

For the third and final attempt to obtain the records, Nephi went alone. He entered Jerusalem and was "led by the Spirit, not knowing beforehand the things which [he] should do" (1 Nephi 4:6).

Before finishing the story, it's important to understand that under the law of Moses, a person in possession of stolen goods could be executed. Remember, Laban accused Laman of being a robber and was going to kill him. Such a thing is considered *justifiable homicide* and not murder, which is the unlawful taking of a human life under the law of Moses:

> If a thief be found breaking up, and be smitten that he die, there shall no blood be shed for him.
>
> If the sun be risen upon him, there shall be blood shed for him; for he should make full restitution; if he have nothing, then he shall be sold for his theft. (Exodus 22:2–3)

Late at night, Nephi found Laban drunk with wine and passed out. Laban was in possession of the stolen gold, silver, and precious things that belonged to Nephi's family. Under the law of Moses, then, Nephi was justified in killing Laban—which he did.

Also under the law of Moses, "if a man lie not in wait, but God deliver him into his hand; then I will appoint thee a place whither he shall flee" (Exodus 21:13). Nephi was told three separate times that the Lord had delivered Laban into his hands. After Nephi killed Laban, the appointed place to flee was into the wilderness by the shores of the Red Sea. In this case, Laban was removed to the Spirit World.

Hezekiah's Problem

Hezekiah's problem was an army of 185,000 that was on its way to destroy Jerusalem.

During the ministry of the prophet Isaiah, the city of Jerusalem was next in line to be conquered by Sennacherib, the king of Assyria. The Lord referred to Assyria as "the rod of mine anger, and the staff in their hand is mine indignation" (Isaiah 10:5). This incident would become a perfect fulfillment of Mormon's prophecy, in which he said, "the judgments of God will overtake the wicked; and it is by the wicked that the wicked are punished" (Mormon 4:5).

Of the forty-plus kings of the Northern Kingdom of Israel and the Southern Kingdom of Judea, only a few were righteous: Jehoshaphat of Judea (about 914 BC); Azariah (also known as Uzziah, about 811 BC); Hezekiah of Judea (about 726 BC); and Josiah of Judea (about 640 BC). Fortunately, Hezekiah was the king at the time Jerusalem was coming under attack. All of the city-states north, south, east, and west of Jerusalem had been conquered. The net was closing in.

The people in the city of Jerusalem needed to repent or be destroyed; there was no way they could deliver themselves. The Assyrians had just finished conquering Lachish, a city-state about twenty-five miles southwest of Jerusalem. Rabshakeh, a representative of Sennacherib, showed up at the city gates of Jerusalem and shouted in the Hebrew language:

> Hear ye the words of the great king, the king of Assyria.
>
> Thus saith the king, Let not Hezekiah deceive you: for he shall not be able to deliver you.
>
> Neither let Hezekiah make you trust in the Lord, saying, The Lord will surely deliver us. . . .
>
> Hearken not to Hezekiah: for thus saith the king of Assyria, Make an agreement with me by a present, and come out to me: and eat ye every one of his vine, and every one of his fig tree, and drink ye every one the waters of his own cistern;
>
> Until I come and take you away to a land like your own land, a land of corn and wine, a land of bread and vineyards.
>
> Beware lest Hezekiah persuade you, saying, The Lord will deliver us. Hath any of the gods of the nations delivered his land out of the hand of the king of Assyria?
>
> Where are the gods of Hamath and Arphad? where are the gods of Sepharvaim? . . .

> Who are they among all the gods of these lands, that have delivered their land out of my hand, that the Lord should deliver Jerusalem out of my hand? (Isaiah 36:13–20)

Isaiah sent a message to Hezekiah saying,

> Whereas thou hast prayed to me against Sennacherib king of Assyria:
>
> This is the word which the Lord has spoken concerning him; The virgin, the daughter of Zion [Jerusalem], hath despised thee, and laughed thee to scorn; the daughter of Jerusalem hath shaken her head at thee. . . .
>
> Therefore thus saith the Lord concerning the king of Assyria, He shall not come into the city, nor shoot an arrow there, nor come before it with shields, nor cast a bank against it. . . .
>
> For I will defend this city to save it for mine own sake. . . . (Isaiah 37:21–22, 33, 35)

Imagine telling the most powerful nation on earth to go jump in the lake. Isaiah used the imagery of a marriage proposal wherein the king of Assyria was the suitor and Jerusalem was the maiden. It would be one thing to tell the king of Assyria a simple no. It was quite another matter to tell the king of Assyria that you despise him and his offer of marriage and that you laugh in his face at the proposal. Nevertheless, that was the message sent to Rabshakeh and to the king of Assyria.

Isaiah acknowledged the prayers of righteous King Hezekiah. The scriptures tell us that 185,000 soldiers surrounded the walls of Jerusalem. One can only imagine the fear that gripped the hearts of the people. Surely a number of them pleaded with King Hezekiah to surrender Jerusalem; at least in the case of a surrender, they would live. A large number of them were probably also repenting and praying to the Lord for deliverance.

The scriptures reported that an angel of the Lord went forth and smote in the camp of the Assyrians the 185,000 soldiers during the night. Sennacherib, the king of Assyria, departed and returned to Nineveh. The angel of death was reminiscent of the Lord as an angel of death passing over the doors marked with lamb's blood in Egypt (see Exodus 12:12–14). In this case, of course, the Lord destroyed the army of 185,000.

Jodi's Problem

Jodi's problem was her toxic mother-in-law, Sally. On a scale of one to ten, with ten being the most toxic, Sally was a twelve.

A *toxic person* is anyone who uses manipulative behaviors and attempts to control others in selfish ways. These people use caustic methods to get others to conform to their expectations. They criticize, nag, complain, use anger, or withhold love and affection as a punishment. They threaten, coerce, and use force to get their way. Toxic people are often emotional blackmailers. They are not above using guilt or fear to accomplish their purposes, and they hold others hostage to their selfish whims and wishes.

You can't please a toxic person. He or she is incapable of giving total acceptance. You will never be good enough. Toxic people dangle acceptance like a carrot on a string. The person who wants to be accepted and appreciated can never quite reach the carrot because toxic people give only partial acceptance. They promise a reward but often deny it, and earned privileges are never secure.

Frequently, toxic people send the message, "I am unhappy. But if you would do this certain thing or behave this certain way, then I will no longer be unhappy." Here is the true message: "I won't be happy no matter what you do because I will find something else that will make me unhappy, and I will have to criticize you about that too." The toxic person's mantra is, *I will be happy when everyone does everything I want done. in the way I want it done. My way is the best way, the only way, and the right way.*

Arnold, Jodi's husband, had grown up in an environment with a toxic mother, and he had developed some defensive skills to cope with his mother. One of five children—three boys and two girls—Arnold had resigned himself to make the best of the situation with his toxic mother. None of Arnold's brothers and sisters would have anything to do with their mother once they were married and out of the house.

Jodi, the daughter-in-law, wanted to please her husband by having a good relationship with toxic Sally. What Jodi failed to grasp was that a relationship involves two parties, and Jodi was only one-half of that relationship. Because they lived in close proximity, Sally expected Arnold and Jodi to come to dinner every Sunday. Jodi always arrived early and offered to help Sally prepare the Sunday meal—and the experience always sent Jodi home in tears. Arnold was used to hearing his mother criticize everyone and everything, and he let his mother's criticism run off his back like the proverbial duck. Jodi, on the other hand, internalized Sally's criticisms and became depressed at the thought of visiting Sally every Sunday. Nevertheless, she endured until they started having children and the children started coming home in tears. With that, Jodi refused to take the children to Sally's home anymore.

At that point, John was asked to help save the marriage of Arnold and Jodi. Arnold couldn't figure out why Jodi couldn't simply ignore Sally's criticisms. Jodi was upset that Arnold refused to protect her and the children from Sally's toxic tirades. Sally manipulated Arnold into accepting responsibility for Sally's high blood pressure, so Arnold was unwilling to upset his mother and risk causing any further damage.

Having written the book *How to Hug a Porcupine*, John was able to introduce skills for coping with a toxic personality. His counsel to both Jodi and Arnold was to let go of the expectation that they were ever going to please Sally. All frustration comes from unmet expectations; if you can change your expectations, you can ameliorate your frustrations.

Chances were good that Sally was never going to change—it was likely that she would go to her grave a toxic person. With that in mind, Arnold and Jodi agreed to a four-step program:

1. They would let go of trying to please Sally without becoming bitter, resentful, and as difficult as Sally (who was the toxic person). Self-preservation was their first responsibility.
2. They would define for themselves what a good person would do in a similar circumstance; they would then establish behavioral goals they knew would please the Lord, knowing the behavior would not please Sally. Pleasing Sally was not their objective; pleasing the Lord was their goal. Adopting this attitude took a great deal of pressure off Jodi. They agreed to pray every night that the Lord would bless Sally while they struggled to maintain a relationship with her.
3. They would always have an escape plan from the toxic person. For example, they could take two cars when they visited Sally. This meant that Jodi could excuse herself, and she and the children could go to a pre-planned alternative activity. Always having an exit strategy was called *Plan B*.
4. Arnold and Jodi would prepare the children to cope. A tool or technique John has successfully used with children who were

exposed to a toxic grandparent was to reward the child who was criticized the most with a double-decker ice cream cone or some other reward. The least criticized children received only a single scoop of ice cream. The children were not to purposely goad the grandparent into being critical, or they completely forfeited any reward. This changed the entire focus for the children. Instead of internalizing the criticism, they simply kept track of it, quietly smiling inside and knowing they had just racked up a point toward their reward.

After about two months of praying for Sally and praying for themselves to do things that would please the Lord in relationship to Sally, Arnold and Jodi were able to be sincerely nice to toxic Sally. Jodi had learned that it was possible to "pray for them which despitefully use you, and persecute you" as taught by the Lord in the Sermon on the Mount (Matthew 5:44). Sally continued being mean to Jodi, but once Jodi changed her expectations from pleasing Sally to pleasing the Lord, Sally's cutting remarks lost their impact. Jodi no longer internalized the negative messages. Jodi treated the experience with Sally as a way to please the Lord. Jodi did not look forward to being with Sally, but came to realize that toxic Sally was the one who had a problem.

Eventually, something extraordinary happened that neither Arnold nor Jodi wanted. Sally had a stroke that left her incapable of speaking. Sally had *aphasia*, a neurological disorder that affected her ability to communicate. Shortly thereafter, a second stroke took Sally's life.

Is it possible that toxic people are placed in our lives so we can learn to be more like Jesus? The Lord removed Jodi's problem, but not until Jodi had learned to please the Lord in her behavior toward her toxic mother-in-law. Maybe the real issue was learning to respond like Jesus. After Sally died, Jodi felt at peace, knowing that she did all she could under the circumstances, instead of having to live with regret and a hard heart.

CHAPTER FIVE

FORGIVING INCREASES OUR ABILITY TO LOVE

There is a power in forgiveness that increases our ability to love. Before we address how forgiveness increases our ability to love, we need to address two important forgiveness issues.

The first involves seeking forgiveness for our own sins. We are expected to go to the Lord with a broken heart and a contrite spirit and to ask the Lord directly through prayer to have our sins forgiven. The Lord is eager to forgive. Baptism by immersion by those with authority represents several things. Chief among them is receiving membership in The Church of Jesus Christ of Latter-day Saints. Another blessing associated with baptism is the washing away of any sins (for those over the age of eight) as we accept the Atonement of Jesus Christ. Following baptism, we can renew the blessing of having our sins washed away as we sincerely repent and worthily partake of the sacrament.

Those who have been excommunicated from the Church are not excommunicated from God. When we joined the Church, we agreed to live by a certain set of standards. When those standards are broken, the bishop, stake president, or other Church leader prescribes a way by which the transgressor can come back into full fellowship as a member of the Church. In this way, Church leaders regulate membership and serve as judges in Israel while the Lord forgives sins.

The Lord said, "I, the Lord, will forgive whom I will forgive, but of you it is required to forgive all men" (D&C 64:10). The second issue, then, relates to the commandment to forgive everyone for every wrong we may have suffered at the hands of others. This includes forgiving others for the hurt, heartache, and sorrow others have caused our loved ones. While we each have individual responsibility for any sin we commit, the commandment to forgive also includes the requirement to forgive ourselves—an important obligation, since guilt robs each of us of the power to love more fully.

Parents of Murdered Children

Probably the most difficult class John ever taught was to an organization called "Parents of Murdered Children." Can you imagine the difficulty of trying to teach a class on forgiveness to those who have suffered such a tragic loss? The group of twelve represented several different religions, and two of them said they did not believe in God at all.

John began his presentation by telling the story of an extraordinary woman; we'll call her Angela. Angela was scheduled to speak on overcoming adversity in an afternoon assembly at our daughter's high school in Mission Viejo, California; John asked the principal for permission to attend, since John thought Angela might be speaking about overcoming drug or alcohol addiction. Imagine 2,400 noisy students waiting in the gymnasium that Friday afternoon, our daughter—a senior—among them. Angela came into the gymnasium accompanied by her two teenaged daughters, and it was obvious she was blind. It then occurred to John that she was probably going to talk about overcoming issues dealing with blindness.

The vice-principal had a real job on his hands trying to quiet down the students, who were excited about that night's football game against Liberty High School and the dance that would follow the game. But when Angela stood up to speak and told her story, the students were spellbound for thirty-five minutes. One could hear the proverbial pin drop.

Angela was graphic to the point of embarrassment. John could see that he was not the only one who was uncomfortable. The principal squirmed a couple of times, but the students were glued to their seats. John mentioned that he was not as graphic as she was when he related Angela's story to the parents of murdered children.

Angela had been shopping at a local supermarket with her two young daughters when she was abducted by a stalker. As she was putting the groceries in the trunk of her car, he knocked her unconscious and threw her in the back of his van. He left Angela's two little girls in the shopping cart.

He took Angela to a motel room where he raped and abused her for several hours; finally, her attacker stabbed her with an ice pick several times and left her for dead. He returned to the motel room, wrapped her naked body in a shower curtain, and hit her head on the door as he tried to carry her body out of the motel room. She groaned. She wasn't dead! He panicked, went to his van, and returned with a snub-nose .32 revolver. He put the gun to her temple and pulled the trigger. She subconsciously raised her head as she was shot, and the bullet took out both of her eyes and the bridge of her nose. The sound of the shot brought several people out of their motel rooms, and the man fled. He was caught and sentenced to twenty years, but served only seven years for aggravated rape and attempted murder. He is now a free man.

Obviously, Angela didn't die, but her adversity was far from over. She went through several surgeries to repair the physical damage. Her husband was not a strong man, and he could not cope with his wife's sexual assault. He abandoned the family.

After a couple of years of counseling and learning braille, Angela decided she wanted to return to the university and finish her degree. Her goal was to become a public speaker, so she completed a degree in communication. Angela graduated with honors.

At the end of each of her presentations, Angela invites a few people from the audience to ask her questions. A microphone had been set up in advance so the students could ask their questions. When Angela invited questions that day in the high school gymnasium, about two hundred students piled out of the bleachers and lined up behind the microphone. After the first question, more than half of them sat down—because they all had a similar question: "How much time do you spend thinking about the man who raped you, and aren't you worried about him coming back now that he is out of prison?" Angela's answer changed our lives:

> I get that question everywhere I lecture. He has taken from me all that he is ever going to take. I am not going to give him my todays or my tomorrows. How many of your todays and your tomorrows do you want to give to the yesterdays that you can do nothing about?

The silence that fell over the assembly was finally broken by 2,400 students simultaneously clapping and crying. Angela wasn't finished. She went on to tell the students that she had done the worst thing to him that she could ever imagine: "I have forgiven him and turned him over to God. I refuse to be a victim. And I will not waste the rest of my life living in regret. Nor will I allow my heart to be filled with hate. My todays and my tomorrows are mine!" The applause went on for several minutes before her daughters ushered Angela out of the gymnasium.

We mean it when we say that Angela changed our lives. John went home and related Angela's story to Bonnie. We determined that day to forgive anyone and everyone who had wronged us in any way. We did not want to give our todays and our tomorrows to our yesterdays. We did not want to live in the land of regret and complaint and victimhood.

We have learned that only two productive things can be done with the past. First, we can learn from it. Second, we can forgive ourselves and others. Almost everything else we try to do with the past is counterproductive.

That was the essence of John's presentation to the Parents of Murdered Children. Later he received several letters thanking him and expressing appreciation for information that changed their lives. However, one professed Christian woman wrote and told him after his presentation that she would never forgive the man who murdered her young son. Her exact words were, "I will go to hell before I ever forgive that man!" John suggested to her that forgiveness did not mean she had to embrace the man who murdered her son. It meant that she turned over to the Lord the responsibility for punishment and judgment for the hurt, heartache, and sorrow the man had caused her.

Lisa Could Not Forgive Herself

In fifty years of counseling, it has been John's experience that many people are stopped dead in their tracks by a challenge such as a divorce or the death of a loved one. John remembers talking to a father of seven children whose wife, Lisa, did not feel they should celebrate Christmas or other special occasions because it was too painful for her following the death of their young son. Lisa felt guilty; she thought that if she had been a better and more attentive mother, her son would not have died. Even if that were true, Lisa had the problem of not forgiving herself.

John asked this father how long it had been since his son had died. It had been seven years. John counseled him to start celebrating these special events immediately.

When John counseled his wife, she said she could not celebrate these events. John tried to be understanding and compassionate. At first, she claimed John couldn't possibly understand—but she withdrew that complaint when he told her our daughter died suddenly at forty-two years of age, and he understood what it felt like to lose a loved one. Lisa was holding the entire family hostage, living in the land of regret and complaint. She had become a prisoner of the past. John asked her to imagine being in the handcart companies of the early pioneers who crossed the plains. He then asked her to imagine that her son had died under those circumstances. Would she bury him? Or would she stay with her son's body, refuse to move on, and possibly lose the rest of her children?

In much the same way, her inability to cope with the loss of her son was destroying the potential positive memories of the rest of her children. John suggested that the rest of the family celebrate these activities. She was welcome to join the celebration or not.

John pointed out that Lisa could do nothing with the past but learn from it and forgive herself. He assured her that the Lord was eager to forgive her and that even if her poor choices made her responsible for the death of her son, she would find the Lord quick to forgive. She was only a sincere prayer away from forgiveness.

Sadly, this story did not have a good ending. This couple divorced because Lisa was unable to forgive herself. Her husband was not willing to subject himself or their six remaining children to living in the land of regret and complaint, to living in the unchangeable past.

Another Great Sin

When I teach classes on forgiveness in a religious setting, such as an Institute of Religion, I ask the students what they believe to be the greatest sin in all eternity. They almost always answer that the greatest sin is the one that leads to becoming a son of perdition, which is correct. Another great sin is not forgiving self and others. The person who chooses not to forgive is telling the Savior that what He suffered in the Garden of Gethsemane does not count. For whatever reason, the unforgiving person feels their personal suffering justifies them in not forgiving themselves or others. They obviously neither understand nor appreciate the Atonement of Christ.

Forgiving is a spiritual issue as well as an emotional one. The victim of a crime, or of an unfaithful spouse, or of molestation carries deep emotional pains that may take years to mend emotionally. It may take a while for us to heal our hearts. However, forgiveness as a spiritual issue means turning judgment over to the Lord. It means removing any feeling of revenge, hatred, or animosity from our hearts toward that person. It does not mean that we have to trust or even like that person.

Trust and forgiveness are two separate issues. The Lord does not expect us to be foolish and unwise. Remember, it is possible to forgive someone and not trust them. Forgiveness does not restore trust, because trust must be earned, and that happens by a person keeping his or her word. The one who wants to be trusted must create a new history of being where he or she said they were going to be and doing what he or she said they were going to be doing. The responsibility for establishing trust rests with the transgressor. We do not need to be "huggy-kissy" with those whom we have forgiven, nor do we need to restore them to their former place in our lives.

We need to be wise in how we interact with those we forgive. It would be foolish to expose an alcoholic to an environment where he had a history of making poor choices; it wouldn't be advisable that a recovering alcoholic take a job as a bartender. Nor would one recommend that a repentant child molester be put in charge of a day-care center. Yes, we are to forgive, but the Lord also expects us to be wise.

Alma proclaimed that "he that forgiveth not his neighbor's trespasses when *he says* that he repents, the same hath brought himself under condemnation" (Mosiah 26:31; emphasis added).

"But his sins are greater than my sins!" you might proclaim. The Lord has one universal standard: "For I the Lord cannot look upon sin with the least degree of allowance" (D&C 1:31). Some sins are more serious than others, but judgment as to what sins are forgiven rests solely in the hands of Christ, who paid for all of our sins in the Garden of Gethsemane.

To be clear, whenever we are reminded of the hurt, heartache, and sorrow we have suffered at the hands of others, we are to say, "Let God judge between me and thee and reward thee according to thy deeds" (D&C 64:11). In time, we can bring ourselves to pray for that person, praying that he or she may find the way spiritually back to God. The scriptures tell us to do what appears to be impossible: "Pray for them which despitefully use you . . . That ye may be the children of your Father which is in heaven" (Matthew 5:44–45).

If we choose not to forgive others, as well as ourselves, we will not have our sins forgiven. "But if ye forgive not men their trespasses, neither will your Father forgive your trespasses" (Matthew 6:15). There is no such thing as atoning for one's own sins, or through vengeance making someone else atone for their sins. No man or woman can self-atone and qualify to have their own sins forgiven.

> Now there is not any man that can sacrifice his own blood which will atone for the sins of another. . . .
>
> There can be nothing which is short of an infinite atonement which will suffice for the sins of the world.
>
> Therefore, it is expedient that there should be a great and last sacrifice . . .
>
> [which] bringeth about means unto men that they may have faith unto repentance. (Alma 34:11–15)

Exodus 20:5 tells us that God is a "jealous God" and when it comes to forgiveness of sin, he is a very jealous God and allows no one but Jesus to hold that power to forgive. "For the Father judgeth no man, but hath committed all judgment unto the Son" (John 5:22)

The Lord stated that regardless of the sins committed against us, if we choose not to forgive, we stand condemned before Him:

> Wherefore, I say unto you, that ye ought to forgive one another; for he that forgiveth not his brother his trespasses standeth condemned before the Lord; for there remaineth in him the greater sin. (D&C 64:9)

When we withhold our forgiveness, we are placing our limited judgment above the Lord's perfect judgment. He has a perfect view of people's hearts and circumstances, and judgment belongs to Him alone. He will ultimately deal out perfect justice and perfect mercy to all—both those who wrong others and those who are wronged. In addition, by requiring us to forgive, the Lord is helping us to choose happiness over misery, to abandon our bitter grudges and resentments, and to receive healing through His grace. Then we discover that, as Elder Kevin R. Duncan of the Seventy has reminded us, "The Savior's Atonement is not just for those who need to repent; it is also for those who need to forgive"[44]

The sin of not forgiving is in a higher and much more serious category than most have understood. It is also where the seventy times seven rule applies. When Peter asked how many times we should forgive an offense, he tried to quantify it with "till seven times?" The Savior responded, "I say not unto thee, Until seven times: but, Until seventy times seven" (Matthew 18:21–22). Elder Neal A. Maxwell taught,

> We can also be too unforgiving, refusing to reclassify others. Yet "he that forgiveth not his brother his trespasses standeth condemned before the Lord; for there remaineth in him the greater sin." (see D&C 64:9.) We cannot repent for someone else. But we can forgive someone else, refusing to hold hostage those whom the Lord seeks to set free!
>
> Ironically, some believe the Lord can forgive them, but they refuse to forgive themselves. We are further impeded at times simply because we have not really been taught why and how to repent.[45]

---

[44] Elder Kevin R. Duncan, "The Healing Ointment of Forgiveness," *Ensign*, May 2016.
[45] Elder Neal A. Maxwell, "Repentance," *Ensign,* November 1991.

President Dieter F. Uchtdorf of the First Presidency explained why extending forgiveness is critical for our spiritual growth:

> Extending forgiveness is a precondition to receiving forgiveness. For our own good, we need the moral courage to forgive and to ask for forgiveness. Never is the soul nobler and more courageous than when we forgive. This includes forgiving ourselves.
>
> Each of us is under a divinely spoken obligation to reach out with pardon and mercy and to forgive one another. There is a great need for this Christlike attribute in our families, in our marriages, in our wards and stakes, in our communities, and in our nations. We will receive the joy of forgiveness in our own lives when we are willing to extend that joy freely to others. Lip service is not enough. We need to purge our hearts and minds of feelings and thoughts of bitterness and let the light and the love of Christ enter in. As a result, the Spirit of the Lord will fill our souls with the joy accompanying divine peace of conscience (see Mosiah 4:2–3).[46]

No one would consciously cast dirt into a sacrament tray and insult the emblems of the sacrament, but not forgiving self and others is casting dirt into the sacrament tray. In essence, you are telling Christ that what He suffered in the Garden of Gethsemane didn't really count and that somehow you are exempt from having to forgive yourself and others. You may think that your personal suffering gives you permission to not forgive. It doesn't. Neither are you justified in punishing yourself or others.

Your attempts to make the guilty suffer will only bring the judgment of God upon you. This does not mean that people are not to be held accountable to the law of the land. Legal consequences and recompense still apply. However, in an imperfect world true justice may not prevail. This makes it all the more important that we let Jesus be the "judge" of both the quick and the dead (see 1 Peter 4:5). Because of the eternal law of justice, every sin will be accounted for.

Consequences of Procrastinating the Forgiving of Others and Self

The choice to postpone forgiving robs us of the ability to love more fully in the present. The longer we wait to forgive ourselves and others, the more

---

[46] President Dieter F. Uchtdorf, "Point of Safe Return," *Ensign*, May 2007.

quality time we forfeit here on earth. Forgiving opens the way for the Holy Ghost to abide with us to a greater degree. There is a soul-freeing power that increases our ability to love that can only be achieved through complete and total forgiveness of everyone for every wrong we may have suffered.

Harboring hard feelings, rancor, and unforgiving feelings requires a tremendous expenditure of emotional and spiritual energy. When we forgive, that energy can be redirected to more positive and healthy behaviors, thoughts, and feelings. We will have more spiritual ability to take our love to our loved ones and our frustrations to the Lord. However, in order to experience anything approaching that kind of freedom requires a total and complete forgiving of everyone.

It may take some time for us to heal emotionally. If we understand that forgiveness does not mean we trust those who hurt us or that we have to restore them to a former position of trust, we can more quickly turn judgment over to the Lord. We can feel confident that Christ will extract the uttermost farthing for those who transgress against us. God will mete out an appropriate punishment on the unrepentant sinner. We want to be on the Lord's side and pray for strength to forgive and trust in the Lord. In the Beatitudes, the Lord reminds us that "Blessed are the merciful: for they shall obtain mercy" (Matthew 5:7; 3 Nephi 12:7.) *Mercy* is defined in part as compassion and forgiveness.[47]

If one asks for forgiveness, we are to forgive him seventy times seven (the Lord's way of indicating a "countless" number). If someone does not ask for forgiveness, the disciple of Jesus is still obligated to forgive him: "And if he trespass against thee and repent not the first time, nevertheless thou shalt forgive him" (D&C 98:41).

Once we understand the seriousness of not forgiving self and others and accept that we are "spiritually" obligated to forgive, our hearts can focus on turning over to the Lord all rights to judge and forgive.

When we think about the wrongs we and our loved ones have suffered at the hands of others, we can find comfort in mentally repeating these words: "I am grateful that my own sins are forgiven as I forgive the sins of others. I will let God judge between me and you and reward you according to your deeds." Those words can bring immediate peace to our souls, even when at times we may have to repeat it several times before we are in control of our unforgiving thoughts.

If not forgiving others is a part of your sins, avoid the tendency to justify yourself. Some might want to obviate their sins by suggesting that their sins are not as bad as those of others, but it avoids the issue of individual

---

[47] See full definition at www.websters.com.

responsibility for any sin. For you or me to grade our sins and compare them to others assumes we have a right to judge. As already established, judgment belongs solely to the Lord. In the hymn "Truth Reflects upon Our Senses," we read, "Jesus said, 'Be meek and lowly,' For 'tis high to be a judge" (*Hymns*, no. 273). Fortunately, it is the Lord's stewardship to judge and not ours. It is in and through the Atonement of Jesus Christ that we can all rejoice and take consolation that those who transgressed against us will be held accountable. We read these sobering words from the Doctrine and Covenants:

> Therefore I command you to repent—repent, lest I smite you by the rod of my mouth, and by my wrath, and by my anger, and your sufferings be sore—how sore you know not, how exquisite you know not, yea, how hard to bear you know not.
>
> For behold, I, God, have suffered these things for all, that they might not suffer if they would repent;
>
> But if they would not repent they must suffer even as I;
>
> Which suffering caused myself, even God, the greatest of all, to tremble because of pain, and to bleed at every pore, and to suffer both body and spirit—and would that I might not drink the bitter cup, and shrink—
>
> Nevertheless, glory be to the Father, and I partook and finished my preparations unto the children of men.
>
> Wherefore, I command you again to repent, lest I humble you with my almighty power; and that you confess your sins, lest you suffer these punishments of which I have spoken, of which in the smallest, yea, even in the least degree you have tasted at the time I withdrew my Spirit. (D&C 19:15–20)

An important issue in magnifying our ability to love in the present is to invite the Holy Ghost to be a greater part of our lives. A bitter and unforgiving heart leaves little room for the Holy Ghost to dwell. There will come a point in our individual progression—during earth life, because of an experience in the spirit world, or during some time in the Millennium—where we will not sacrifice the joy of the companionship of the Holy Ghost for the short-term pleasure of any sin. This includes whatever satisfaction we may gain from not forgiving. The temporary pleasure of sin may involve dishonest monetary gain, illicit sexual pleasure, or supporting our pride by lying, cheating, or not forgiving. There will come a time when the temporary pleasure of any sin succumbs to every knee bowing and every tongue confessing that Jesus is the Christ and that the joy of the companionship of the Holy Ghost is greater than the temporary pleasure of any sin.

We will acquire some of these life lessons about learning to live with the Holy Ghost from the consequences of poor choices and an afflicted mind. The change will come from inside our souls. The sooner we learn to value the companionship of the Holy Ghost in this life, the greater will be our ability to love and to be a disciple of Jesus in the here and now. In the words of the scriptures,

> And if a person gains more knowledge and intelligence in this life through his diligence and obedience than another, he will have so much the advantage in the world to come. (D&C 130:19)

The advantage is one of personal growth and of having overcome issues that others will yet have to overcome. The other advantage is a greater ability on our part to love those who mean the most to us now.

The word *gospel* literally means "good news." Now comes the good part of the good news. The good news is that when you turn accountability for sin over to the Lord, you are free to pursue a happier life. When you release justice, vengeance, and punishment and place them in the hands the Lord, you cast a heavy burden off your back. Let the Lord take responsibility for the wrongs we and our loved ones have suffered so He can exact justice in His own time and in His own way. We are then free to focus on our todays and our tomorrows and not be held hostage to our yesterdays. Maybe the most important issue is being able to love those you care about the most that are still within your sphere of influence today.

The good news continues. By surrendering forgiveness to the Lord, one escapes from living in two very sad places. One place from which you escape is the land of victimhood. Every person who chooses to be the victim of the wrongs he or she endured, even legitimate wrongs suffered at the hands of an evil person, puts himself or herself in the position of seeking sympathy. Being a victim requires that you live in the past and seek sympathy from others in the present or inside the prison of your own mind. There is also the danger that in seeking sympathy one uses it as an excuse and justification for not taking charge of the good he or she can still do in the present.

Whether consciously or not, victims find themselves telling and retelling the story of how they were the victim of a divorce, crime, or bad behavior of someone else or they replay their victimization over and over in their minds. Sympathy requires that one live continually in a past over which he or she has no control. The mindset of a victim is to seek sympathy. Sympathy is a poor substitute for happiness. The sympathy seeker avoids seeking happiness in the present, preferring to live in the woes of the past.

The other land from which we escape when we forgive is the land of vengeance. The Lord has made it clear throughout the scriptures that "To me belongeth vengeance, and recompence" (Deuteronomy 32:35). It is not our responsibility to become vigilantes or avengers of the wrongs we or others suffer.

We believe that men are "accountable for their acts" and "crime should be punished according to the nature of the offense" (D&C 134:1, 8). It is consistent with gospel teachings that we can forgive a thief, but the thief may still have to deal with the broken laws of the land and suffer the consequences of his thievery. It is prudent to remember that we live in an imperfect world where a good but imperfect justice system cannot render perfect justice. This is why it is important to hold people accountable but realize that only the Lord can determine and require that the unrepentant transgressor pay the "uttermost farthing." Once we have sought for accountability through the laws of the land, it is imperative that we let go of the injustice by turning "recompense" over to the Lord. Everything else that we do with the past will only lead to depression and a cankered soul or to playing the role of the unempowered victim or vengeance seeker.

Let's say that the person we are talking about does indeed forgive everyone, including herself or himself. The next step is to pray that the person you have forgiven will repent and that Heavenly Father will prepare the way for him or her to become her highest and best self. Once we find ourselves praying with all our hearts for those who would spitefully use us, we are in tune with Heavenly Father's plan for all His children (see Matthew 5:44–45).

This attitude cannot be developed overnight. It will take time. It is unrealistic to think that we can suffer a betrayal and instantly take a Pollyanna attitude. When we forgive, it does not mean that we cannot grieve for the violations that befall us. It means that will turn judgment and justice over to the Lord while our hearts mend.

We need not worry that anyone will ever get away with anything, for through the Atonement of Christ every sin is accounted for and no unclean thing or person can enter the kingdom of heaven. All will repent except the sons of perdition. Some will repent on earth, some will repent in spirit prison, and some will repent during the Millennium. They will repent of their own free will, even if "It must needs be, by the things which they suffer" (D&C 105:6). Some will suffer even as Christ suffered in the Garden of Gethsemane before they are forgiven of the hurt, heartache, and sorrow they inflicted on others. After they have paid the "uttermost farthing," they will be set free only as they come forth clean and repentant, having suffered for their sins, and having forgiven everyone.

It would be a mistake to assume that because people suffer for their unrepentant sins on earth or in hell that they have self-atoned. The Atonement of Jesus involved a perfect sacrifice of His life as well as suffering for sin.

> For it shall not be a human sacrifice; but it must be an infinite and eternal sacrifice.
> Now there is not any man that can sacrifice his own blood which will atone for the sins of another. (Alma 34:10–11)

The laws of eternal justice required a sinless sacrifice that only Jesus could make and for which he was foreordained as the "lamb without blemish and without spot: Who verily was foreordained before the foundation of the world" (1 Peter 1:19–20).

But why wait to forgive or why have to go through the valleys of victimhood or vengeance and endure all that unnecessary personal suffering and mental anguish involved in not forgiving? We have already discussed the invitation from Jesus to "Come unto me, all ye that labour and are heavy laden, and I will give you rest. . . . and ye shall find rest unto your souls" (Matthew 11:28–29).

It is our firm conviction that we are on this earth to join with our Heavenly Father in committing our whole souls to bringing to pass the immortality and eternal lives of our brother and sister spirits. We do that through forgiveness and love. However, our ability to love is impaired when our hearts have not forgiven ourselves or others. It is an absolute truth that an unforgiving heart is limited in its ability to love.

We have personal testimonies that as we have forgiven everyone that has offended us or our loved ones, and turned the transgressor over to Jesus, we have found peace. Now the imperfections we still possess can more completely focus on serving the Lord and praying for those who are waiting for us to love them. This attitude and disposition pleases the Lord. It empowers us to ask others to forgive anything we have done to offend them or to hurt them in any way. It is now up to them to forgive us or not, but we can always pray they will forgive us for their own sakes.

Another part of our testimony is the tremendous burden that was lifted from our souls when we felt that our own sins had been forgiven because we had forgiven others. When that happened, we realized that we had held the Lord hostage from forgiving us of our sins. The greatest trade we ever made in this life or throughout all eternity was, and will be, to forgive others so that our own sins could be forgiven.[48]

Just because you forgive does not mean that you won't have occasion to remember the wrongs against you. It will be how you choose to remember those wrongs that matters. It has been helpful for us to say, "Thank goodness for the Atonement of Jesus Christ, that our sins and the sins of our loved ones can be forgiven as we forgive others."

The essence of forgiveness is turning judgment over to the Lord and letting go of personal animosity. We challenge each of you to experience this same peace that can be realized only by following the Lord's commandment: "I, the Lord, will forgive whom I will forgive, but of you it is required to forgive all men" (D&C 64:10).

---

[48] John L. Lund, *For All Eternity* (American Fork: Covenant Communications, 2008), 128–129.

CHAPTER SIX

HOW DO I LOVE THEE?

LEARNING TO SAY *I LOVE YOU* in the love language of your loved one is an acquired skill. When we want to demonstrate positive and loving feelings, most of us treat our loved ones like we would like to be treated ourselves. The problem is that our loved one might want to be loved differently. There are several books on the market discussing love language. John wrote one of the first books on love language when he was in graduate school at the University of Washington, and it was published in 1987.[49] It was titled, *Avoiding Emotional Divorce*. The essence of the book was that people get emotionally divorced before they get legally divorced. Staying emotionally married requires that we learn each other's love language. At "drlund.com" you can access quizzes and take the love language test. The test is also in the appendix of this book. There are twenty-seven questions that if honestly answered will give you a strong indication of what your love language is.

For ease of understanding, I prefer looking at three basic love languages: touch, verbal, and visual. A person's love language is defined by the way he or she sends and receives messages of acceptance, affection, and appreciation. It covers the total range of caring responses.

The Hand, The Ear, and The Eye

Touch-oriented people enjoy the complete range of physical expression. The hand symbolizes all touching experiences. Holding hands, hugging, and being physically close communicate acceptance, affection, and appreciation.

Verbal-oriented people are excited about sharing their feelings. Talking and listening remain paramount. The ear and the mouth are the central focus. Heart-to-heart talks, caring words, and meaningful discussions comprise the love language of the verbally centered person.

---
[49] John L. Lund, *Avoiding Emotional Divorce* (Salt Lake City: Hawkes Publishing, 1987).

Visually centered people often define their values in terms of results and accomplishments they can see. Achievement is very important. Hard work, status, or things often become the measure of their self-worth.

Most people are not solely touch, verbal, or visual. Most of us tend to be a combination of these, with one of them being more dominant. John recommends you take the love language quiz in the appendix. The objective of the quiz is to help you improve your skills in more effectively communicating acceptance, affection, and appreciation.

Learning to express your love in the love language of your loved one is only half of the challenge. The other half is to control your negative communications.

The Horseshoe Magnets in John's Office

Over the years, John has used a pair of horseshoe magnets to teach the principle of attraction and rejection. Certain behaviors attract, and other behaviors repel.

To profess that you love someone and want them to love you in return as you display a consistent pattern of unhealthy negative behaviors, feelings, and thoughts toward that person betrays reality. Loving behaviors attract and consist of acceptance, affection, and appreciation messages.

Occasional and rarely given reproof or properly given criticism may be justified. Twenty-five years ago, Dr. John Gottman at the University of Washington taught that at least five positive communication signals need to be given for every negative signal.[50] When that ratio is not maintained, the relationship is doomed to conflict, alienation, and abandonment.

As a general rule, you should use five times as many words to confirm the person's worth to you as you do in giving criticism. Following is a typical criticism of a teenager given by a frustrated mother:

> I want you to know, Mary, that I really love you, but you need to pick up after yourself and not leave your clothes scattered throughout the house. It's not fair to me or others that we should have to pick up your clothes. You need to be more responsible. It's very important that we take care of our own things.

---

[50] John Gottman, *Why Marriages Succeed or Fail* (New York: Simon and Schuster, 1994), 56.

In this example, there were ten positive words before *but*. Those were followed by fifty negative words. That needs to be turned around. If you don't turn it around, you have no real intentions of changing behavior, and you are willing to have to repair the damage later. Be aware that venting your frustrations will almost always be seen as a negative. You will be perceived as the one having a problem, even if what you're saying is true.

Here's what the five positive words to one negative word ratio might sound like when talking to Mary about picking up her scattered clothes:

> Mary, I was just thinking that when I was your age, I didn't have all the social pressure that young people have today. You seem to handle social pressure so well while still maintaining your values. I'm really proud of you. You are a great example for your brothers and sisters. The bishop pulled me aside last Sunday and told what a good influence you were on the young women in our ward. He asked me if I had a secret in how I raised you. I told him the truth: It isn't me. It's you. You have always had a strong desire to please your Heavenly Father. Keep it up; you're making me look really good. Seriously, I appreciate and love you, Mary.
>
> I do have one request that is not too painful. It would mean a lot to me if you would pick up your clothes and not leave them scattered around the house.

In this example, there were about twenty-two words expressing criticism and one hundred twenty-six words showing appreciation. That is a five-to-one ratio of positive over negative words. Communicating this way takes practice and determination. It is a skill, and like any skill, it takes practice. Bowling is a skill. Beginners throw a lot of gutter balls before they're able to knock down all ten pins or pick up a spare.

Before you become discouraged and despondent because you realize that you are human, consider the end goal. You can be an instrument in the hands of the Lord to influence your loved one, and you become a better self.

Examine the list below of positive and negative behaviors. Honestly evaluate the types of messages you are sending; see where you can increase more positive messaging and where you might be able to limit or eliminate negative interactions.

Positive Behaviors That Attract	Negative Behaviors That Repel
Acceptance	Frustration
Acknowledging	Ignoring
Adequacy	Inadequacy
Affection	Rejection
Approval	Disdain
Assurance	Blame, Accusation
Confidence	Ineptness
Emotional Support	Emotional Withdrawal
Encouragement	Discouragement
Equality	Inequality
Faith	Doubt
Goodwill	Hostility
Happiness	Sadness
Hope	Disappointment
Intimacy	Control
Mutuality (common consent)	Manipulation (one-sided)
Order	Confusion
Partnership (cooperation)	Competition
Peace	Anger
Reinforcement	Criticism
Respect	Trivialize
Security	Fear
Serenity	Conflict
Sustain	Berate
Trust (when there is no evidence to mistrust)	Mistrust
Validate	Negate
Pleasant	Contrary
Approving	Judgmental
Negotiation	Arbitrary

We all are born into a world of conflict that is filled with both good and evil. There are clear choices to be made. It is also true that at some point we will fall short of the person we would like to be. However, when you recognize the power for good that you can be, it will not be a sacrifice to give up the negative. You will be able to look back and see that you have removed an obstacle that was keeping you from being the loving person you truly desired to be.

There are several versions of an old song made popular by Bing Crosby called, "Ac-Cent-Tchu-Ate [Accentuate] the Positive." It is easy to find on YouTube. The main lyrics support a wonderful theme, which is to accentuate the positive and eliminate the negative. Furthermore, modern prophets have taught this as a message of the gospel. President Gordon B. Hinckley exemplified the kind of attitude we should all possess in his address to students at Brigham Young University:

> What a wonderful time to be alive. How enthusiastic I feel. . . . I hope you are enthusiastic, because there is a terrible ailment of pessimism in the land. It's almost endemic. We're constantly fed a steady and sour diet of character assassination, faultfinding, evil speaking of one another . . . In our homes, wives weep and children finally give up under the barrage of criticism leveled by husbands and fathers. Criticism is the forerunner of divorce, the cultivator of rebellion, sometimes a catalyst that leads to failure. Even in the church it sows the seeds of inactivity and finally, in many cases, apostasy. . . .
>
> I'm suggesting that we accentuate the positive. I'm asking that we look a little deeper for the good, that we still our voices of insult and sarcasm, that we more generously compliment virtue and effort. . . . You are partakers of the gospel of Jesus Christ . . . The message of the Lord is one of hope and salvation. . . . [L]ook above and beyond the negative, the critical, the cynical, the doubtful, to the positive.[51]

Most pessimists consider themselves realists, which is their justification for being critical and negative. Giving one's self permission to be a realistic-pessimist runs counter to the teachings of modern-day prophets. It was President Thomas S. Monson who bore a fervent testimony about the

---

[51] Gordon B Hinckley, "The Lord Is at the Helm," Fireside Address, BYU Marriott Center, Sunday, March 6, 1994.

importance of sharing loving words and of having a positive outlook towards life. He reminded the members of the Church, "There are hearts to gladden. There are kind words to say."[52]

In a discourse at Utah Valley University, Elder M. Russell Ballard reminded the students that it was their responsibility to be disciples of Jesus Christ: "'You have to keep a very positive, upbeat outlook in life' he said. Rather than having a 'woe is me' or 'things aren't working the way it should' attitude."[53] President Russell M. Nelson taught:

> Saints can be happy under every circumstance. We can feel joy even while having a bad day, a bad week, or even a bad year! My dear brothers and sisters, the joy we feel has little to do with the circumstances of our lives and everything to do with the focus of our lives.[54]

How do we survive in a worldly environment that is constantly sending negative and often evil messages?

On one occasion, John was interviewed for a Church assignment by President Harold B. Lee. At the conclusion of the interview, President Lee asked if John had any questions. He did. He asked the President how he managed to avoid evil thoughts in our society. His answer was instructive and helpful. President Lee said that it was impossible to live in this world and not be exposed to evil thoughts. He went on to say that it was not evil to have an evil thought, it was only evil to choose to dwell on the evil thought. He then volunteered how he handled "bad thoughts":

> I have memorized the words of a Longfellow poem and several of our lengthy hymns, including all seven verses of "A Poor Wayfaring Man of Grief." When I have an evil thought, I immediately begin reciting either the poem or one of the hymns. Sometimes I've had to go through a hymn more than once before I was in control of my thoughts. I have found the counsel of James 4:7 to be true: "Resist the devil, and he will flee from you."[55]

The melody of the song "Ac-Cent-Tchu-Ate the Positive" is quite catchy and easy to sing. John has followed President Lee's counsel and used that

---

[52] "The Gifts of Christmas," *Ensign*, December 2003.
[53] M. Russell Ballard, Orem Institute of Religion, October 30, 2015.
[54] Russell M Nelson, "Joy and Spiritual Survival," *Ensign*, November 2016.
[55] Notes from personal interview with Harold B. Lee.

song as one of his tools to combat negative thinking. Feel free to use this song or any other positive, uplifting poem or hymn that will assist you in controlling that critical thought or unkind word.

A wonderful quartet called the Mills Brothers sang a song titled, "You Always Hurt the Ones You Love." You can also find them on YouTube. The words are sad but often true:

> You always hurt the one you love,
> The one you shouldn't hurt at all;
> You always take the sweetest rose
> And crush it till the petals fall;
>
> You always break the kindest heart
> With a hasty word you can't recall,
> So if I broke your heart last night,
> It's because I love you most of all.

Justifications for Uninspired Criticism

"Everybody does it."

"What's the big deal, anyway?"

"After all, criticism is how we learn to grow."

"Haven't you ever heard of constructive criticism?"

Frankly, there is no such thing as constructive criticism. *Construction* means to build up. Make no mistake: criticism tears down; it does not build up. Tearing down and building up are two separate processes. One can go up in an elevator and one can go down, but you cannot do both at the same time. In the same way, it's not possible to give constructive criticism. This is why it is so necessary that we learn how to give *appropriate* criticism.

When we commit to controlling our negative communications and make sincere efforts to do so, we will find fewer broken hearts and fewer unkind words we can't recall. The journey of a thousand miles begins with one step in the right direction. Are you willing to take that first step?

Try the 24-Hour Challenge

For everyone who wants to escape the addiction of criticism, the twenty-four-hour challenge is a place to begin. For twenty-four consecutive hours, refrain from criticizing anything, anyone, or even yourself. It isn't as easy as it sounds, but it is not impossible. When you slip, start the twenty-four hours over again. One man to whom John gave this assignment moaned, "It will be forever before I get this right."

Unless it is a life-or-death situation, abstain from all forms of criticism. This includes sarcasm, uninvited opinions, analysis, appraisals, evaluations, insights, questions that imply criticism, direction giving, or contrariness. For some, employment requires people to be critical; these would include people in jobs like building inspectors, supervisors, police, or quality control. These special cases are exempt only if the criticism is justified, asked for, and you received permission to criticize—and the criticism must relate directly to your work.

Otherwise, you must abstain from all criticism for twenty-four hours. The majority of people do not succeed the first time they try; only about one in every two hundred are able to do it within twenty-four hours. Do not be too discouraged if you must start over again thirty or forty times. Frankly, it took John three weeks before he was able to successfully complete this assignment. He made it for more than twenty hours on several occasions but discovered that when he got behind the wheel of a car, he become critical of other drivers. On the day he successfully completed twenty-four hours of not saying one critical word to anyone about anything, he made it a point not to drive. Bonnie was able to complete this assignment in one week. Our experience is typical. Remember the moment you slip and criticize, the twenty-four-hour period starts over again. Do not criticize self, spouse, children, parents, coworkers, the boss, the government, or dumb drivers.

What About Nonverbal Criticism?

You are probably wondering, "If I think it but don't say it, does it count against the twenty-four hours?" If a critical thought enters your mind and you get rid of the thought in a moment or two, then it does not count and you do not have to start your twenty-four hours over. If, on the other hand, you let that critical thought stay in your mind and it develops into a frown, or you are marching around slamming doors or murmuring to yourself, then yes, you have to start over again.

"It's Harder Than I Thought"

One lady who was given the twenty-four-hour challenge looked puzzled for a moment. She glanced up at her husband, who was standing by her side, and said, "Okay, I'll try to go for twenty-four hours not criticizing or dwelling on a critical thought." Then, pointing to her husband, she said, "But he will never make it!" After a pause, she said, "Oh dear, I have to start my twenty-four hours over again, don't I?"

Her husband did not verbally respond. However, he frowned at her, and a slight sneer formed at the edge of his mouth. He also pointed his finger at her in a mocking manner. This, of course, was nonverbal criticism. John pointed out to him that nonverbal criticism was also a reason for him to start his twenty-four hours over again.

The two of them walked off muttering, "This is going to be harder than we thought."

"Yes," John said, "overcoming a lifelong habit of criticizing is hard, but, like overcoming most addictions, it is worth it."

Those Who Made It Twenty-Four Hours Without Criticizing

In one study involving more than eight hundred people, after three days only twenty people had been able to go for a period of twenty-four hours without criticizing. They were permitted to count sleeping time as a part of the twenty-four hours! The responses from those who made it were interesting.

"It was easy," said one woman. "My husband and son were out of town."

Another woman said she used a technique from a seminar she had attended where everyone wore a rubber band around the wrist. Each time they broke the rules of the seminar they snapped the rubber band. She was able to meet the twenty-four-hour challenge because every time she had a critical thought, she snapped the rubber band and didn't give voice to her criticism.

One man in the group observed, "I was so criticized as a child that I decided I would not be a critical adult."

Another man suggested that we form an organization called CA—Critiholics Anonymous—and that we hold weekly support meetings. He said that he was taught to go for a walk before he said something critical. His statement was reminiscence of what President David O. McKay did when he was tempted to criticize his wife. He went for a walk. He said he went for a lot of walks.[56]

One mother reported that after she had gone twenty-four hours, her teenage daughter, unaware of her mother's commitment not to criticize, asked if she was feeling okay.

Why Should I Try Not to Be Critical?

Why should you try to stop criticizing? There are several answers to this question; here are some of the more important ones:

- To lay the foundation for love instead of rejection.
- To increase the number of positive interactions.
- To be more effective in communicating.

---

[56] CES Banquet John attended where President McKay made that statement; those in attendance laughed.

- To reduce unnecessary conflict.
- To experience greater peace and harmony in all relationships.
- To not become a toxic personality avoided by others.

What Are the Lessons I Should Learn by Abstaining From Being Critical for Twenty-Four Hours?

- Become aware of your compulsion to criticize.
- Gain greater awareness of the critical nature of those around you.
- Experience the power of self-mastery.

It is unrealistic to believe that you can go the rest of your life without saying anything critical. There is such a thing as appropriate criticism. As discussed at the beginning of this book, there are two things necessary in giving appropriate criticism. First, you must be in emotional control of your feelings and thoughts and your criticism must be directed by the Holy Ghost. Second, how you deliver the message is as important as the message itself. The criticism must be focused on the behavior or the choice being made by your loved one and not on your loved one's worth. More important than your criticism will be your ability to separate the worth of the individual from the deed you are criticizing.

All criticism is directed at changing behavior. Uninspired criticism changes things for the worse. Criticism poorly given breeds alienation and rejection. Make no mistake about the critical message you are sending. You are telling someone that you do not approve of his or her behavior. About 99.9 percent of the time, the one being criticized will interpret your critical message as a rejection of him or her, not of a behavior. This is why it is so important to separate the critical message from the worth of the individual.

A good thing to do with each relationship is to ask the other person, "If I had something critical to share with you, how would you like me to do it?"

Here are some suggestions about how to manage criticism:

Have a set time every night or once or twice a week when you will go over your criticisms. This gives both parties an opportunity to prepare to hear a negative message. It removes the temptation to express your criticism while you are emotionally upset or frustrated.

Another option is to write the criticism down or put it in a text message after agreeing mutually that writing it down is acceptable to both parties. The advantage to writing it down in a letter or a text is that the person can read the critical message without having to deal with the critic's body language or tone of voice. Doing so allows the person to focus on the message and not on the messenger. *Warning!* Both parties have to agree in advance, and you shouldn't send numerous critical text messages per day.

Another suggestion for dealing with criticism is to tell the person that you have a criticism you would like to share. Would now be a good time, or would the person like you to talk about it later? This is an approach we used with our own eight children. Four of those children wanted to know the criticism right then; the other four were willing to wait until the Millennium. That wasn't an option, of course; we agreed to talk to them later that night, and they naturally hoped we would forget.

A common response from fathers and mothers is that they do not have time to criticize properly. They only have time to point out the criticism and the needed change in behavior. When John hears that, he asks them when they will have time to repair the damage done by just focusing on the criticism.

Is There Any Hope for Me? Trina and Robert

Trina was a raging critiholic and had been all her life. She grew up under a constant barrage of criticism. After fifteen years of marriage, her husband, Robert, left her and sued for custody of the children. Because Robert had tape-recorded his wife yelling unmercifully at the children, the judge awarded all five children to the father.

During the ninety-day waiting period for the divorce to be final, Trina realized she was going to be out on the street without a husband and without her five children. She pleaded and importuned her husband to go to a marriage and family counselor. He agreed.

When Robert and Trina showed up in John's office, the woman was desperate and in a state of panic. It took John twenty minutes just to calm her down. Finally, the story unfolded. She had been molested as a child. Her mother was toxic. Her father was a workaholic and never available to the family. The dysfunction seemed endless and was all too familiar. After she finished what was, in essence, a justification for her tantrums, John asked her if she wanted understanding or solutions.

"Trina, you are about to lose your husband and your five children," John said. "Do you believe in the power of the human spirit to change? Do you believe that an individual has the ability to overcome a terrible background and to choose to live a better life?"

"I want to believe that," she said, "and I am willing to do anything to save my family."

"Trina, I want you to stop criticizing this very moment," John told her. "For one whole week I want you to not say one critical thing—not one word. If you are unwilling to follow my counsel or if you fail, I will not continue to be your counselor."

Then I turned to her husband. "Robert, if this marriage relationship fails you are going to have sole custody of these children, and your wife will only be allowed to have third-party visitation."

"That is my understanding from what the judge said," replied Robert.

"My point is that you are going to have the full responsibility of correcting and guiding these five children. I would like you to begin now with this new assignment. In other words, if anything of a corrective or disciplinarian nature needs to be said, I want you to do it. I want Trina released from all expectations of criticizing, changing, or disciplining the children—zero expectations of criticizing."

John went back to Trina. "Trina, do you really understand what is required of you? I am asking you to quit cold turkey, 100 percent, zero tolerance. If you fail even once, it's over. Do you understand, Trina? In less than ninety days that is going to be your role anyway. You have nothing to lose and a family to gain."

We went over the list of negative and unattractive behaviors. They all described her childhood. She wept and began to go into a pity party and degrade herself. John stopped her abruptly and told her, "Trina, you can't criticize yourself, either. Don't go there. Stop it this very minute. I don't want you to criticize anymore. Don't criticize yourself, your husband, your children, not one word. Do you understand?"

She quickly dried her tears and said, "Yes. Yes, I understand."

"If it's negative, don't say it," John requested. "Please repeat the assignment."

Trina retorted, "I am not to criticize myself, my children, or my husband—not even one word."

"Yes," he said, "that is the first part of your assignment. The second part of your assignment is to go home and love your children. Spend a few minutes each day with each child, doing a loving, bonding thing with each one. If that is too overwhelming, then take one child a day and focus on doing a loving thing with that child."

They left the office with an appointment to come back in a week and report on the progress. A week later, they returned to John's office. Before Trina could sit down, she burst into tears. They were soul-rending sobs! John was fearful that she had failed in her attempt and this would be their last meeting. John asked Robert if she had failed in her assignment of not criticizing.

He looked surprised. "No," he said. "She was great. We had a wonderful week. It was the best week of our married life for me and for the children. We all got along great. I handled all the problems, and she was amazing. I could live the rest of my life with that Trina. I didn't believe when we left the office last week that she could do it, but she did."

Trina was still crying. After a time, she gained sufficient composure to cry out, "You don't understand! You don't understand!"

"What don't I understand?" John asked.

Between her sobs she blurted out, "I don't know how to love! I don't know how to love!"

Trina thought that mothers criticized and gave direction. Repeating what she saw in her own home as she grew up, she thought criticizing was a loving behavior. Seeing that the children did what she thought they ought to do was her understanding of loving. When Trina couldn't criticize, she didn't know what to say. She didn't know how to express love. She lacked the most basic skills in communicating acceptance, affection, and appreciation.

Trina was right. She didn't know how to love. We spent the next several weeks teaching Trina how to love—how to communicate acceptance, affection, and appreciation to her children and to her husband.

That was several years ago. Trina and Robert and the five children stayed together and were very functional and quite happy with life. After not having seen them in more than four years, John asked Trina if she was ready to learn an appropriate way to communicate criticism. She became very serious and said, "I'm never going back there again—not ever." Since she and Robert were happy and doing well in their relationship, John decided to drop it.

The story of Trina is a real story. Sadly, there are a large number like Trina in the world. Criticism is so much a part of everyone's life that it is difficult to discuss it in a sane and rational way. Trina was actually surprised that criticism was a core issue in her relationships. How criticism is managed is a core issue in every relationship.

A Key Issue

Our quest to take our love to our loved ones and to take our frustrations to the Lord requires that we manage our critical natures. Forgiving and loving messages are best given and received when they are given separately and apart from one another. If that can't be done, then using the Gottman 5 to 1 positive to negative messaging is the next best approach. If it is our desire to be an instrument in the hands of the Lord as a "love agent," our words and behaviors have to be consistent with that objective.

Sharon and Her Abusive Spouse

When John saw Sharon for the first time she was confused and depressed about her relationship with her husband, Jerry. His words and behaviors did not match. Anger management was an issue for Jerry. He often flew into a rage. Jerry expected Sharon to support him in every decision, even though she was not a part of the decision-making process. When Sharon thought Jerry was being arbitrary with the money, with the children, or with her, she asked for justification.

When they were first married, Jerry reacted by slamming doors or walking away from the relationship. As time went on, his negative behaviors escalated into cursing, swearing, and belittling Sharon. When these actions didn't work in silencing Sharon, he began pushing her, pinching her, and slapping her. These behaviors sent Sharon into tears and terrified the children. Later Jerry apologized, told Sharon he loved her, and promised never to do it again. However, he did do it again—and again.

Sharon was confused because Jerry's words did not match his behaviors. Under these circumstances, John counseled Sharon not to believe words but to believe only behaviors. Jerry and Sharon faced several critical issues. It is one thing to experience a singular event where anger resulted in verbal abuse. There should be zero tolerance for physical abuse. Anyone who is physically abusive must be removed from the home, be required to take lessons in anger management, and be required to demonstrate behavioral change when he or she returns to the home. The verbally abusive person must be willing to see a professional counselor. Both members of the relationship must learn how to manage the negative in their lives in healthy ways.

The lesson that Sharon had to learn was that physically abusive behaviors trumped loving words. Sharon was focusing on the words and not on the behaviors. When Sharon evaluated Jerry's behaviors as evidence of being loved, she realized that Jerry's words of love were shallow and self-centered. Jerry didn't perceive Sharon as an equal. Jerry expected Sharon to be an obedient child. His rage and anger were tools that he used to manipulate and control Sharon. I explained to Sharon that Jerry's love was very much conditional upon her acting as a child. She was not loved or appreciated or valued as her own person.

For about three weeks, Jerry ameliorated his behaviors; finally, though, he reached the boiling point, his rage turned into physical abuse, and he slapped Sharon. Following my counsel, Sharon called 911, and the police removed Jerry from the home. Jerry promised to change his behavior, but he had broken all his previous promises and lacked credibility. In lieu of divorce, Jerry agreed to complete an evening course in anger management that John taught at a local community college. Additionally, Jerry and Sharon attended an eight-week course in marriage communication skills and communicating in the love language of your mate.

It was three months before Jerry left the basement apartment of his brother, where he had been living, before returning home to live with Sharon as an equal in their relationship. This story had a positive outcome, but many do not. Some people are trapped in a generational cycle of abuse.

Break the Cycle

There is a wonderful organization centered in Orem, Utah, called Chain Breakers. Their objective is to break the chain of abused children becoming abusive parents themselves. They also focus on teaching their patrons how to appreciate and stand up for themselves. They do great work. Over the years, John has spoken to this group several times.

Learning to judge another's love for them by their behaviors and not by their words was a difficult lesson for those who were in abusive relationships. Abused people often give more credit to words than to behavior. One of the most common responses to John's suggestion that behaviors trumped words was, "But he said he loved me!"

When we define love as attraction, appreciation, acceptance, and affection behaviors, it becomes easier for people to see the difference "where actions speak louder than words."

Managing the negative communications you receive from others is compounded by the fact that you are not perfect. The abusive person uses your imperfections as justification for his or her abusive behavior toward you. Don't buy it. Don't let the abusive person convince you that you deserve to be abused because you are the reason he or she is unhappy, frustrated, or abusive. Abusive people are masters of transferring responsibility for their behaviors to others.

Most people who are on the receiving end of verbal and physical abuse feel some level of responsibility for the abusive person's behavior. This is a fundamental flaw in their thinking. It goes against the eternal truth that we are all accountable for our behavior regardless of the behaviors of others. Physical abuse should not be tolerated. Consistent verbal abusive or a pattern of verbal abuse is a sign of a toxic personality. People who feel trapped in an abusive relationship should seek strength from the Lord and pray for divine intervention while availing themselves of a professional counselor and organizations like the "Chain Breakers" or The Church of Jesus Christ of Latter-day Saints Social Services.

Our Sincere Desire

It has been our sincere desire in writing this book that knowledge of correct principles in human behavior will inspire some to stop giving uninspired and inappropriate criticism. Our experience is that focusing on forgiving increases our ability to love. Understanding the love language of a wayward loved one will increase our effectiveness to communicate love in a way he or she can appreciate. These are all things that we can do independent of anyone else.

Equally important is the reality that our Heavenly Father will divinely intervene in the lives of our loved ones. We can actually bind the Lord to a promise. Our part of the contract requires that we cease finding fault one with another except as inspired by the Holy Ghost. It will require patience on our part, and we must trust that the Lord's timeline may include post-mortal experiences. We have witnessed divine intervention in the lives of our loved ones. We have seen hearts softened and people strengthened physically, emotionally, and spiritually. We can testify that the Lord will raise up others to do what we cannot do, and that He will lead people away from an impossible situation and ultimately even remove the problem itself. All of this is possible if we take our love to our loved ones and our frustrations to the Lord.

APPENDIX

LOVE LANGUAGE QUIZ[57]

1) What statement best describes you?
a. A deeply feeling person
b. A talkative-sharing person
c. A doing-showing person

2) As a child, the thing I remember receiving most was . . .
a. Affection
b. Verbal praise
c. Rewards

3) My family of origin demonstrated love . . .
a. By touching
b. By telling each other
c. It was just understood

4) As a child I remember being . . .
a. Spanked
b. Yelled at
c. Grounded

5) People need to be more considerate of . . .
a. Other people's feelings
b. How they speak to each other
c. Other people's time and schedules

---

[57] From the book *For All Eternity* by Dr. John L. Lund; www.drlund.com.

6) In communicating affection to my mate, I prefer to give . . .
a. Tender kisses
b. Tender words
c. A gift of tender meaning

7) I would most enjoy receiving from my companion . . .
a. A hug and a kiss when we meet in the evening
b. An opportunity to talk about the day's events
c. A phone call during the day

8) For a small gift I would most enjoy receiving . . .
a. A coupon that said, "Good for one back rub or foot massage"
b. A personal, handwritten letter expressing appreciation
c. Working with me on a project

9) I am most frustrated by . . .
a. Insensitive people
b. Critical people
c. Unfair people

10) I need to spend time with my mate talking about . . .
a. Positive things
b. Significant events and others
c. Alternatives and solutions

11) I would prefer . . .
a. Quietly walking hand in hand
b. A positive heart-to-heart talk
c. A clean house or well-kept yard

12) It is more important to have my mate . . .
a. Be with me; sit next to me
b. Talk about my hopes and dreams
c. Remember to run an errand for me

13) I would rather . . .
a. Be embraced and treated affectionately
b. Be told I am loved
c. Be shown that I am loved

14) What I admire in a friend is . . .
a. Unconditional acceptance
b. Availability and understanding
c. Loyalty and dependability

15) I would prefer to have my mate . . .
a. Reach out and touch me
b. Say, "I love you"
c. Surprise me with a good deed

16) My idea of a great weekend is . . .
a. Spending time just being together
b. Visiting with friends and family
c. Getting lots of projects accomplished

17) I would prefer receiving appreciation by . . .
a. A hug
b. A kind word
c. Receiving something I need

18) With which of these statements do you most agree?
a. I would rather hold hands in public, or walk arm-in-arm, and mean it, than live in a fancy house.
b. I would rather be told I was loved, than be married to a workaholic who is always giving me everything but him/herself.
c. You shouldn't have to tell somebody you love them all the time; they should know it by the way they are treated.

19) The thing that upsets me most about children is . . .
a. Not being affectionate
b. Talking back
c. Not being obedient

20) The thing that upsets me most about my loved one is their . . .
a. Lack of intimacy
b. Failure to communicate
c. Lack of responsibility

21) I would rather have my mate . . .
a. Be physically expressive and touching
b. Recognize my efforts with words of appreciation
c. Demonstrate their appreciation by doing something I can see

22) When I get upset as a parent, I would be more inclined to . . .
a. Spank
b. Scold
c. Withdraw privileges

23) As a parent of a young child I would prefer . . .
a. Holding or wrestling with them
b. Reading a story to them
c. Taking them to the park

24) I feel good . . .
a. Just being held
b. Being able to fully express myself
c. Getting things done

25) Which statement best describes you . . .
a. Physically expressive
b. Verbally expressive
c. Accomplishment oriented

26) As a sign of caring for me I would like to receive from my loved ones . . .
a. Lots of affection
b. Sincere praise
c. "Hands on" help

27) I would prefer to have my mate . . .
a. Spend more one on one time with me
b. Pay me a compliment
c. Show greater participation in doing the daily tasks

After you have answered all the questions, add up your totals for *As, Bs, and Cs.*

Total *As* _____ Total *Bs* _____ Total *Cs* _____

- If you answered *A* more often than any other, you are Touch-Oriented.
- If you answered *B* more often than any other, you are Verbally-Oriented.
- If you answered *C* more often than any other, you are Visually-Oriented.
- If you have a close balance of *As, Bs,* and *Cs,* you are known as a Universal Donor. (Universal Donors need to have a balance of Touch-, Verbally-, and Visually-Oriented messages.)

If a person is clearly a Touch-, Verbally-, or Visually-Oriented person, it would be easier to learn their love language. Most of us are a combination of these characteristics, although one will tend to emerge as a dominant characteristic of a person's love language. People change and adjust in many ways, but often maintain the same basic love language.

It becomes important to understand your loved one's love language and to communicate with them in that language. It is unrealistic and unproductive to expect them to change their love language.

Of course, your loved one has a responsibility to learn your love language as well and to communicate with you in that language.

Love Language Defined

A person's love language is defined by the way they send and receive messages of acceptance, affection, and appreciation. It is how one says or understands, "I love you; I accept you; and I appreciate you."

The Eye, the Ear, the Hand

Visually-Oriented people often define their values in terms of accomplishments—in other words, what the eye can see. Achievement is very important. Hard work, status, or things often become the measurement of their self-worth.

Verbally-Oriented people are excited about sharing their feelings. Talking and listening remain paramount. The ear and the mouth are the focus. Heart-to-heart talks, caring words, and meaningful discussions comprise the love language of the Verbally-Oriented.

Touch-Oriented people enjoy a complete range of physical expression. The hand symbolizes all touching experiences. Holding hands, hugging, and being physically close communicate love to this person.

An interesting twist to the golden rule applies to learning someone else's love language. We will usually treat others the way he/she wants to be treated by others.

The Art of Translation

Today it's possible to access the internet and translate anything into any of a dozen languages. When it comes to "love language," the art of translation is recognizing that your loved one is telling you they love you—in their love language. It may not be how *you* would like your loved one to communicate acceptance, affection, or appreciation but it is their "native language." Rather than resent your loved one for using a language different from yours, translate their caring responses into appreciation. At the same time, you can express that you would also like your loved one to learn to speak your love language.

You will probably never be as good as someone else in speaking their love language, nor will they necessarily be as good as you in communicating your love language. It's the effort that counts. Becoming bilingual in love languages enhances both parties in a relationship.

Defining *Enough* Is Vitally Important

When will the touch-centered person have touched enough?
Never!
When will the visual- or task-centered person have done enough?
Never!
When will the verbally-centered person have talked enough?
Never!

It is important to understand what is *enough* for any given day. That can be accomplished by owning your expectations. As easy as this may sound, most people find it difficult to ask for what they want. They hope the other person will remember everything that is important to them. That's an unrealistic expectation, and it sets up a loved one for failure—as well as frustrating the one with the expectation.

Let's look at what it means to own your expectations in the present.

Sam came home every day from work, announced he was home, and went to watch the news on TV. June wanted him to come home and greet her with a hug and a kiss. She had mentioned how important that was to her, but Sam usually forgot. John told June that since it was her expectation, she needed to own it in the present. When Sam came in the house and said, "I'm home," June needed to respond by saying something like, "I'm glad you're home; now come and give me a hug and a kiss and then go and watch the news."

Confronted with this scenario, June might ask, "Why can't he just remember? It doesn't mean as much if I must ask every time."

If June doesn't want to ask, she's setting Sam up for failure and convincing herself that Sam doesn't love her just because he doesn't remember. However, if Sam is willing to be a great responder and June is willing to be a great initiator, her expectation can be met every day.

How much talking is enough? What about a phone call during the day, or how about exchanging one or two text messages? What about talking for fifteen minutes every night before you go to bed in addition to your normal interaction?

How much touch is enough? Maybe the hug and kiss will be enough for that day. If not, the one who needs the touch should be willing to say, "It would mean a lot to me if you would hold my hand when we are walking together." Or, "Come and sit on the couch and hold me for a moment."

Once again, unwillingness defeats all solutions. If someone is brave enough to own their expectations in the present, the other party should not see themselves as inadequate or failing, but as great responders. It is the responsibility of the one who has an expectation to own it and communicate it in the present. If this is going to work, it's critical to define enough—and the definition should be agreed to by both parties.

It's easy to become discouraged and depressed when you feel inadequate. If you give everything and it is not enough, you may ask why you should give anything at all. Defining *enough* is defining adequacy for today.

More About the Visually-Oriented Person

A visually-oriented person is one characterized by the value they place on accomplishments, work, possessions, or things. In other words, what you do "to" that person is not as important as what you should do "for" him/her. For a visually-centered person, actions speak louder than words.

Visually-oriented people are prone to compartmentalize their lives. For them there is a time and a place for everything as well as for every relationship. They are often organized and sequential. They are inclined to make lists, establish budgets, and live by the appointment book. However, because of their greater expectations, visually-centered people can experience greater frustration. They are inclined to be perfectionists or are frustrated if they are not.

There is a tendency for visually-centered people to overcommit themselves in terms of what they can realistically accomplish in a day, a month, or even a lifetime. They are high achievers, and their expectations for others are also great.

The love language of visually-oriented people is largely defined by what they can see accomplished. Here's an example of how that works:

Mark came home every day asked his wife, "What did you *do* today?" A person who is not visually-oriented might have asked a different question, such as, "What kind of a day did you have?'

Mark's wife, Sally, had spent the day running errands, doing general clean-up, and engaging with a friend in a two-hour phone call to help her friend with a problem. Sally felt a sense of accomplishment in helping her friend through an emotional crisis, but Mark was upset when he learned that Sally had spent that long on the phone. To Mark's way of thinking, talking didn't count. As far as he was concerned, his wife had wasted her time and could have accomplished more productive things.

Sally responded by calling him an insensitive _____. "You don't want me as a person," she exclaimed. "What you want is a cook and a maid."

Mark saw love as a simple matter: You show someone you love them by hard work and effort toward common goals.

John counseled Sally about the "art of translation."

"Mark does love you, Sally," John explained. "What he is calling into question is your love for him. He wants to see your love translated into action. For example, you could ask Mark, 'What could I do for you today that would mean the most to you?'"

If Sally asked Mark that question, he might give Sally a list of seven things:

1. Cleaning the house
2. Buying the ingredients to pack his lunch
3. Having something to eat in the house
4. Being dependable and on time for appointments
5. Running some errands for him
6. Working side by side on a project

7. Giving him a surprise gift with a note expressing appreciation for his hard work

Given that list, Sally should say to Mark, "Which one of the seven is the most important for you today? I'll try to do more than one, but I'll make a special effort to do your number-one choice."

When John explained that to Sally, she said, "It sounds like he wants me to be a slave!"

"There is a difference between service that is motivated by love, and service that is based on intimidation, force, or coercion." John explained. "Mark would like you to do things because you love him and because you are trying to please him. Service is seen as an expression of love, not servitude. Mark is frustrated because he believes that you do not love him and that you do not appreciate his efforts on your behalf. He is willing to work sixteen hours a day in order to provide you with tangible signs of his affection. When he comes home at night and asks you the question, 'What did you do today?' what is he really asking?"

"I don't know," said Sally, "but I feel like I am being put on trial every night. I get to a point where I dread having him walk through the door."

"Would it make any difference," John asked, "if Mark walked through the door and said, 'Sally, I love you. Do you love me?'"

"Yes," she said.

"In a very real way, that is exactly the intent of Mark's question," said John. "Mark is asking if you love him in his love language."

"But what about my needs?" Sally asked.

John pointed out that teaching someone a foreign language is difficult, but it is done every day by willing people. John explained that Sally can teach Mark her love language by owning her expectations in the present and by defining what enough will be for that day.

The List

Bonnie, a visually-oriented mother of four small children, was consistently after her husband, John, to fix all the little things that always needed fixing around the house. Because John was not a handyman, he didn't even have the inclination to fix things.

To avoid nagging him, Bonnie proposed that a list of the things that needed to be done be kept on a sheet of paper attached to the refrigerator door. Over a period of weeks, the list became longer and longer until a second, third, and finally a fourth sheet was added. Every time John got something out of the refrigerator, he was reminded of the mountainous number of "little things" he needed to do. Finally, he decided to spend two hours every Saturday fixing things, but the list continued to grow, and the two-hour period on Saturdays proved inadequate to make even a small dent in the list.

One Saturday, to his wife's surprise, a hired handyman showed up and asked to see the list. John had told him to start at the top of the list and work until he was done. He was not to question the tasks, just do them. John took the children to a football game, and when they returned home in the evening, all the work on the "little things" was done.

At first, Bonnie was somewhat upset with John because she felt it wasn't fair. Her expectations were not only that the "little things" be done, but that John do them—that was his role, and to have someone else take over was cheating. However, after talking it over, John and Bonnie decided it wasn't important who did the work as long as it got done. Now Bonnie says, "Bring on the handyman!" and John gladly does exactly that.

More About the Verbally-Oriented Person

A verbally-oriented person is one who places great value on the word as a primary channel for communicating love, acceptance, and appreciation. Sometimes it is quite possible to be verbally-oriented and thought of as a "quiet type." It is not so much about the *quantity of words* as it is about the *quality of caring words* the person uses or needs.

Most talkative people, however, are verbally-oriented. One of our very verbal daughters used to sit on the end of our bed and talk and talk until both of us fell asleep. Even then, she was still talking.

Here's a great example: A frustrated woman who was very verbally-oriented destroyed a mink coat. It was her husband's gift to her for their twenty-fifth wedding anniversary.

"I have told you a thousand times," she said, throwing the coat at him, "I don't want things from you. I want you to tell me that you love me. In twenty-five years, you have told me that you loved me only five times."

Incredible as it may sound, she named the five dates, including the day, the month, and the year.

"I admit it," said the husband, "I am a quiet man. It embarrasses me to talk about loving someone. In my home, as we were growing up, I knew I was loved. Nobody had to tell me all the time. It was just understood. My wife and I live in an exclusive part of town, she has a maid, and she has everything she wants. I am always giving her gifts. How can she question my love?"

John counseled the verbally-oriented woman to learn the art of translation. She was to translate her husband's task-oriented disposition into verbal communication. Every time her husband gave her something, she was to repeat out loud or in her mind, "I have just been told that I am loved."

The husband, in turn, was advised to continue to give gifts because it pleased him. But he was also to be willing to say, "I love you," when he gave the gift. If it embarrassed him to say it in front of the children or others, then he was to take his wife off to a private corner every day and tell her that he loved her.

Kim was a verbally-oriented twenty-six-year-old who was married to a strong, silent type. Her husband was content, but Kim was depressed much of the time. She expected to be told daily that she was loved, just as her mother had been told by her father.

John talked to Kim about the art of translating. "How does your husband tell you he loves you?" he asked.

"By being a good provider," she replied.

"Every time he leaves for work this next month, say to yourself, 'Thank you for telling me you love me by how hard you work.'"

After a month, her depression had fled because her expectation had been met by learning the art of translation. Kim also learned to own her expectations in the present, just as Sally had to with Mark.

Verbally-Oriented People Are Often Their Own Therapist

Most verbally-oriented people have a greater need for someone to listen to them than to talk to them. They are looking for sounding boards. Frequently, they need to talk through each alternative, even though the person listening might already have the solution to the problem. Many people need to talk over each alternative to satisfy themselves that their decisions are sound, and when they are cut off, they are frustrated. It requires patience on the part of the listening person to give 100 percent attention and to demonstrate understanding. Verbally-oriented people are often their own therapist, and they will work through the problems and insecurities if there is someone who will listen.

One of the best ways to develop the art of listening is to develop the ability to keep others talking. Sometimes, just being quiet is not enough. Research indicates that people who are encouraged to verbalize begin, in a matter of minutes, to give positive, feeling-level responses. If the person continues to verbalize and reaches a positive feeling level, then it is more likely you can deal with the real issues.

The ability, or the skill, to reach the level of positive feeling is developed through the art of active listening. As a measure of your ability to be an active listener, see how long you can keep someone talking. As an experiment, select someone—a friend, a relative, one of your children, or even a total stranger—and see how long you can keep that person talking. If you're stumped on how to do that, try one of these suggestions:

1. Ask questions that cannot be answered with a "yes" or a "no" or with a single word. For example, "Where are you from?" can be answered by saying," Denver," and that's the end of the conversation. Ask questions that will stimulate thinking: "What do you think?" "What is your opinion?" "How do you feel about…?" "Why do you feel…?" "Why do you imagine they would do that?" "What are you going to do now?" "How did all this happen?" It is difficult to answer questions like these with a "yes," a "no," or a single word.
2. Nod your head if you understand what the person is saying or ask the person to explain if you don't. If you agree with what is being said, encourage the person by adding one- or two-word comments such as, "That's true," "I agree," or "Isn't that usually the case?"
3. Appropriate eye contact is helpful in developing the art of active listening, but staring at someone is considered impolite. In fact, staring without moving your head is a body language signal often interpreted as hostility, disagreement, or resistance. If you want to stimulate and encourage conversation, especially on a positive-feeling level, you need appropriate eye contact. Interrupt occasionally with a direct question. such as, "What do you mean?" and look at the person. When they respond, maintain eye contact and nod your head.
4. Don't fold your arms, cross your legs, or lean back when someone is talking to you. These are all non-verbal turnoffs. Subconsciously, the folding of your arms acts as a barrier. Leaning back indicates withdrawal. Crossing your legs is frequently a way of showing disinterest. When sitting, lean slightly forward,

clasp your hands, and let them rest in your lap. This is a sign of openness and encourages the expression of feelings. If you are standing, face the person and let your arms rest at your sides
5. Don't stand or sit too close to the person. Respect personal space.
6. Touching your face with your hand from time to time indicates contemplation, thought, and meditation.
7. Be honest and sincere. If you aren't sincere, active listening is meaningless in achieving a level of positive feeling.

Reaching a Positive Feeling Level

While studying for a master's degree at the University of Washington, John was assigned to go home and see how long he could keep Bonnie talking. He went forth armed with newfound active listening skills, ready and anxious to engage in an exciting adventure. It was about 4:30 p.m. when he arrived home. The children had already returned from school, and Bonnie was in the kitchen preparing the evening meal.

After some small talk about the day, John leaned across the counter, looked intently at Bonnie, and began asking her thought-provoking questions. At first, she looked surprised. Quickly, however, she began to express her thoughts. He nodded his head, maintained appropriate eye contact, and interrupted occasionally to have her expand on a feeling or an idea.

John soon discovered he had a tiger by the tail. Once Bonnie began expressing herself and reached the feeling level, she moved to sharing some of her innermost desires, frustrations, and concerns. The floodgates were opened, and a veritable ocean of feelings came pouring out. The noise of the children faded into the background, and two and a half hours later John collapsed, emotionally drained. But Bonnie seemed to be getting stronger, her mind more invigorated. Then, as she finished the one-sided conversation, she said something that was both humorous and instructive: "That was the best conversation we've had in a long time."

More About the Touch-Oriented Person

Imagine for a moment that you could not see, hear, or speak. Touching would instantly become your all-important medium of communication. You would send hundreds of messages that would communicate many different feelings, all through touch.

Most people are acquainted with touch-oriented people who are viewed with some suspicion because they are always touching. Jean, for example, was a touch-oriented woman who was also very talkative and outgoing. When she saw friends, male or female, she approach them, take their arm, and give them a squeeze. In fact, most friends were fortunate if they could escape without also being hugged.

In a marriage relationship, it is a good idea to agree that unless there is a clear verbal understanding that sexual intercourse is the objective, all touching is an end in itself. Not all hugging and kissing have sexual overtones. In European families, greeting one another with a kiss on the cheek or both cheeks is expected. There are many families where hugging and kissing between brothers and sisters or parents and children is a common mode of expression. Many touch-oriented people come from these kinds of environments. A touch, a hug, or a kiss is intended to be a whole and complete message within itself and not a means to an end. In fact, holding hands or walking arm-in-arm with a spouse are great communicators and can be an end in itself. Most touch-oriented people sincerely appreciate it when their mate sits next to them in public as well as in private instead of sitting across the room or being separated by the children. It is not always practical, but it is always appreciated.

If you are married to a touch-oriented person, make it a practice to discreetly and softly touch your spouse's arm or shoulder as you pass by, whether your spouse is in the kitchen, sitting in a chair, or walking down a hallway.

All the examples used in describing love language have dealt with couples. However, the principles apply to parent-child relationships as well as to relationships between friends and those between co-workers. What we are really discussing is empathy. We are striving to understand how others communicate acceptance, affection, and appreciation. The more effective we can be in owning our expectations and appreciating how others value words, deeds, or touch, the more effective we will be able to take our love to our loved ones and our frustrations to the Lord.

ABOUT THE AUTHORS

Dr. John L. Lund has authored thirteen books, numerous CDs, and has served as a Registered Family Counselor in Washington and Idaho. He has worked within the Utah and California judicial systems as an Alternative Dispute Resolution Provider (ADRP) specializing in resolving conflicts in healthy ways. He attended both the University of Washington and Brigham Young University; his graduate and post-graduate specialty has been interpersonal communications. Dr. Lund has been referred to as the "Doctor of Communication" on various TV programs and has lectured in fifty-seven different countries on four continents. The Catholic Church sponsored Dr. Lund and his wife, Bonnie, for two years with a series of lectures in Australia and New Zealand on resolving conflicts in healthy ways.

As an active member of The Church of Jesus Christ of Latter-day Saints, he served a mission to Mexico; served as a bishop in his hometown of Olympia, Washington; and served as a bishop in the Moscow Idaho 1st Ward. In Logan, Utah, he was a counselor in a stake presidency. For thirty-six years he taught for the Church Education System in the capacities of an Institute instructor and adjunct professor at Orange Coast College in Costa Mesa, California, UC Irvine, the University of Washington, the University of Idaho, Utah State University, and the University of Utah. Dr. Lund was the director of the Institute of Religion in Washington, Idaho, and at Utah

State University in Logan. He likewise served as an area administrator for eastern Washington and northern Idaho. For more than thirty years, he taught for the BYU Campus Education Week program as well as the Know Your Religion programs throughout the United States and Canada.

Currently, he teaches the gospel doctrine class in Sunday School and is an ordinance worker at the Jordan River Temple. He says that his best decisions in life were "choosing to be a disciple of Jesus Christ and marrying Bonnie."

BONNIE JEANNE GERTSCH LUND WAS raised in beautiful Midway, Utah, where she was a "Swiss Miss" for the annual Swiss Days and valedictorian of Wasatch High School. She attended BYU on scholarship and maintained straight A's in chemistry. BYU is where she met and married John. They have been married for fifty-six years, and she has typed every book and manuscript that he has written, including this one, which she coauthored. She and John are the parents of eight children, twenty-three grandchildren, and four great-grandchildren—with more on the way. She has served in various callings in Primary, Young Women, and Relief Society, and she currently serves as compassionate service leader in the Murray Utah 16th Ward.

She has traveled with her husband for more than fifty years, and together they present real-life communication challenges. The CD series "For All Eternity" was recorded in front of two stakes, and audience interactions can be heard as they practice problem-solving. John freely confesses that Bonnie is the wind beneath his wings. Recently, Elder and Sister Lund completed a senior couple mission teaching the women inmates at Timpanogos Prison and the men at Utah State Prison. Both Bonnie and John have led and lectured on forty tours to Israel, Egypt, and Jordan as well as seventeen tours to Machu Picchu in Peru and numerous trips to China, Southeast Asia, and all of Europe. Their combined wealth of knowledge about these different cultures adds to the wisdom of why, when dealing with the difficult to love, we need to take our love to our loved ones and our frustration to the Lord.